D1562427

Squatters and Oligarchs

Squatters and Oligarchs

Authoritarian Rule and Policy Change in Peru

DAVID COLLIER

The Johns Hopkins University Press
Baltimore and London

HD 555
C 65

Manufactured in the United States of America

The Johns Hopkins University Press, Baltimore, Maryland 21218
The Johns Hopkins University Press Ltd., London

Library of Congress Catalog Card Number 75-34112
ISBN 0-8018-1748-X

Library of Congress Cataloging in Publication data
will be found on the last printed page of this book.

For Stephen and Jennifer

Contents

Figures and Tables

Acknowledgments

I would like to express my gratitude for the many kinds of assistance, both institutional and personal, that made it possible to complete this book. The principal period of field work in 1968–69 was supported by a Latin American Teaching Fellowship. Through this fellowship I was fortunate to have the opportunity to be associated during my stay in Lima with the Instituto de Estudios Peruanos, whose director, José Matos Mar, and staff assisted me greatly in my work. Supplementary field work in August and September of 1972 was supported by the Latin American Studies Program of Indiana University and a brief visit in August of 1974 was made possible by a travel grant from the Social Science Research Center. The Center of International Studies of Princeton University provided a congenial environment in which I carried out the final work on the manuscript.

Many people in Peru contributed to the progress of my research. Jorge Reyes, Dale Nelson, and Fernando Calderón provided indispensable help in carrying out the interviews for the survey of settlement formation. This survey would not have been possible had it not been for the willingness of present and past community leaders in the settlements to devote many hours of their time to responding to numerous detailed questions about how their communities were formed. Officials in government offices concerned with problems of housing, as well as private individuals who had worked in this area, also provided valuable assistance. In particular, the staff of the Oficina de Barrios Marginales of the Junta Nacional de la Vivienda and Marcia Koth de Paredes of PLANDEMET generously shared data on squatter settlements and insights on housing and settlement problems. Francisco Codina of the Survey Research Center of the Peruvian Ministry of Labor kindly provided access to two survey studies which form the basis of part of the analysis in Chapter II. The Newspaper Clipping Archive of *La Prensa* was an invaluable source of data on the history of settlement formation and settlement policy.

Julio Cotler, Sinesio López, and Giorgio Alberti offered warm friendship and hospitality, broad intellectual guidance, and numerous practical suggestions during my stay in Peru. Philippe Schmitter, Guillermo O'Donnell, and Julio Cotler have played a central role in shaping my understanding of Latin American politics and in contributing to the development of the arguments presented in this book. I am greatly indebted to Theodore Lowi for introducing me to public policy analysis and for sharing his contagious sense of intellectual excitement about studying politics. Abraham Lowenthal made a decisive contribution to the research through the Peru Seminar which he organized at the Center of Inter-American Relations in New York in 1973. The book would never have taken its present form were it not for his great skill as a critic and editor and the opportunity to develop the analysis which was provided by the seminar. Alfred Stepan and Henry Dietz made a number of helpful suggestions and kindly drew on their own field work in squatter settlements to fill me in on periods of policy in the 1970s on which my information was incomplete.

In addition, a number of other colleagues either commented on drafts of the manuscript or offered suggestions and comments about the project which have been helpful in completing this research. These include Susan Bourque, Peter Cleaves, Alfred Diamant, Edward Epstein, Fernando Fuenzalida, Howard Handleman, Carl Herbold, Alex Inkeles, Jane Jaquette, Robert Kaufman, Anthony and Elizabeth Leeds, Sherman Lewis, William Mangin, Patricia Marks, Joan Nelson, Liisa North, Scott Palmer, Luis Soberón, John Turner, and Douglas Uzzell. I of course remain solely responsible for errors or limitations in the analysis. Princeton University Press, the Transaction Press, and the Center for International Studies of the Massachusetts Institute of Technology kindly granted permission to use in this book material previously published by them in article form.

Finally, my wife, Ruth, shared with me the fascinating experience of getting to know Peru, the excitement of piecing together a research project, and also the hardships of data analysis and of the many times when things got bogged down. She has also read and insightfully commented on more drafts than either of us cares to remember. For these many kinds of assistance, I lovingly thank her.

David Collier

Princeton, New Jersey
July 1975

Selected Dates in Recent Peruvian History

1945   The Apra party is legalized. Bustamante y Rivero elected president in coalition with Apra. Apra wins majority in congress

1947   January 7:   Assassination of Graña
           January 12:   General Odría enters cabinet

1948   October 3:   Attempted coup by a faction of Apra
           October 27:   Military coup. General Odría assumes presidency

1956   Prado elected president

1962   June 10:   Presidential election. No candidate has the necessary one-third of the votes. Election goes to Congress.
           July 18:   Military coup. General Pérez-Godoy is first president under the military junta, follwed by General Lindley

1963   Belaúnde elected president

1968   October 3:   Military coup. Velasco assumes presidency

1975   August 29:   Velasco removed from presidency

Squatters and Oligarchs

Modernization and Political Change

Early in the course of the research that led to this book, I was confronted by an intriguing question from a Peruvian friend: How is it possible that in a country that has been as oligarchic and authoritarian as Peru there could be such a massive growth of squatter settlements around the nation's capital?[1] The settlements stood in stark contrast to the charm of old Lima, violating all conventional norms of aesthetics and planners' standards. Formed through the apparently illegal seizure of land, they seemed to represent an affront to the system of private property which was the basis of the power of the landed oligarchy. The settlements had generally been viewed by the established classes of Lima as a "belt of misery" and a breeding ground of political radicalism which threateningly surrounded the city and which, in some dimly imagined political upheaval, could dangerously cut off the capital from the rest of the country. How is it possible that more than a quarter of Lima's population had come to live in such neighborhoods in a country that had, until the military coup of 1968, so tenaciously protected itself from change?

Social science research—both Peruvian and North American—had, not surprisingly, reached more sophisticated conclusions regarding the settlements than were reflected in traditional stereotypes in Lima.[2] It was recognized that in a context of massive urbanization and massive urban unemployment and underemployment, settlements provided solutions to many problems of low-income migrants. The settlements offered free land, rent-free housing, an opportunity to build and improve homes, and opportunities for community development based on self-help which do not exist in conventional low-income housing. In order to obtain the benefits offered by settlements, low-income migrants willingly fought the

3

established system to occupy and retain the land on which they founded their communities. A partial answer to my friend's question is thus to be found in the tenacity and hard work of the squatters themselves.

This book attempts to provide a more complete answer, based on a large body of new data on settlement formation collected from interviews in settlements and from archival sources. It is shown that one of the most important causes of the appearance of settlements in Lima has been the extensive, though often covert, support of the Peruvian elite and the Peruvian state. In particular, members of the oligarchy, and political leaders who have represented their interests, have been directly involved in encouraging the formation of settlements. Settlement formation has literally been a game of squatters and oligarchs in Lima. A major purpose of this analysis is to explore the extent of this elite and state involvement, the types of governments and of political groups that have been involved, and the reasons for this involvement.

Public Policy and Elite-Mass Relations

At the same time that the data provide answers to relatively specific questions concerning the evolution of settlements in Lima, they are also relevant to a broader theme that has been of growing importance in recent research on Latin America—the role of public policy as an independent factor in shaping elite-mass and state-society relations. To a substantial degree, these relations depend on levels of economic modernization, on patterns of social and political mobilization, and on the autonomously developed structure of political groups in any particular society. In addition, however, public policy plays a central role in shaping them. Governments commonly attempt to mold elite-mass relations to fit the economic and political interests they represent and, correspondingly, to fit their ideological conception of the appropriate means of ordering political relationships in society.

The particular pattern of elite-mass relations that the state attempts to promote in any society is, of course, rarely static. Rather, in the course of economic and social modernization, it evolves with the evolution of the interests that the state represents and with the appearance of new and changing crises with which the state must deal. In nations such as Peru, in which the form of elite-mass relations may be characterized as predominantly authoritarian, one would therefore expect economic and social modernization to produce a series of stages or subtypes of authoritarian rule. The examination over time of policy toward elite-mass relations would therefore be a useful means of analyzing these subtypes. Somewhat surprisingly, however, relatively few studies—either of Peru or of other Latin American countries—have analyzed the evolution of authoritarian rule over extended periods of time, and even fewer have carried out this analysis with a specific focus on the evolution of distinct subtypes of authoritarian rule.[3] This book seeks to carry out this kind of analysis by examining the evolution of public policy toward one aspect of elite-mass relations—the relationship between the state and urban squatters in Lima.

A number of features of the Lima settlements make settlement policy an appropriate focus for such an analysis. The settlements are numerically important, with a population of roughly a million, representing over a quarter of the population of greater Lima and a far greater proportion of the urban poor. Because the Peruvian coast offers an unusually favorable geographic and climatic setting for settlement development, the potential for improvement of individual homes and community facilities that exists in any settlement is particularly great in Lima. Since small amounts of state aid can greatly increase the level of self-help activity in settlements, settlements have long offered opportunities for aiding the poor in which virtually every government has shown great interest. Settlement policy is thus a natural place to look for evidence concerning the type of relationship that each government wishes to promote between the state and the urban poor.

The analysis of the evolution of settlement policy in Lima is organized into eight chapters. Following this brief introductory section, the present chapter provides an overview of the types of questions that may usefully be raised about the relationship between economic and social modernization and political change in a conservative, authoritarian setting such as Peru and summarizes certain crucial economic, social, and political transformations that have been occurring in Peru in the twentieth century. These transformations are viewed as the underlying cause of the patterns of policy change that are the focus of this study. Chapter II introduces the basic issues of settlement policy in Lima, focusing on the characteristics of Lima settlements and on the linkages between settlement policy and the several related areas of policy that are of particular relevance for understanding settlement policy: policy toward urbanization, housing, poverty, property, and toward the political incorporation of the urban poor.

Chapter III explores the different types of settlement formation that have occurred in Lima, devoting particular attention to the previously neglected role of the Peruvian state. It seeks to demonstrate that the state has played a major role in encouraging the formation of settlements in the capital and to identify certain major transitions in the evolution of the state's role. Chapters IV through VII trace the development of public policy toward settlements and settlement formation from 1948 to 1975. These chapters explore four distinct periods: the period of paternalism, the liberal period, the period of party politics, and the period of military rule from 1968 to 1975. It will be shown that the particular combination of economic and political interests that were represented in each government and the way in which these interests interacted with a series of political crises led to distinctive choices in each period regarding settlement policy—regarding the strategy for linking the settlement residents to the state that was reflected in settlement policy and regarding the way in which settlement policy was used to deal with problems of urbanization, agrarian reform, poverty, property, and housing. A concluding chapter places the evolving patterns of settlement policy in comparative perspective and draws together the analysis of the relationship between economic and social modernization and policy change in Peru.

Modernization and Political Change

In exploring the links between policy change and modernization in an authoritarian setting, this book addresses certain broad questions concerning the relationship between economic and social modernization and political change. It must be emphasized at the outset that the political consequences of modernization considered here are quite distinct from those that were widely discussed in social science literature in the later 1950s and the 1960s. Among the writers who adopted the "prerequisites" approach that was common in that period, it was frequently argued that as industrialization, urbanization, communications development, middle-class growth, and other modernizing transformations occurred in Third World countries, there would occur a growth of democracy and a decline of authoritarianism in the political sphere.[4]

The Democratization Thesis

This thesis appeared to be firmly grounded in three types of evidence. First, the developmental pattern which it posited represented a repetition of the pattern of political modernization followed by North Atlantic countries that Barrington Moore, Jr., has characterized as having taken the "democratic route" to modernity.[5] In these countries social and economic modernization was, in fact, accompanied by growing political equality and democratization, and it was often believed that the countries of the Third World could follow a similar developmental path.[6]

The second empirical basis for this thesis was the striking cross-sectional correlation between political democracy and economic and social modernization that was reported in numerous studies during the 1960s, both for Latin America and elsewhere.[7] The longitudinal inference often made from this relationship was that with economic growth and social modernization, many Third World countries could eventually achieve stable democracy.

Finally, this thesis also appeared to be supported by the fact that the 1950s and early 1960s were unquestionably a period of democratization in the Third World. In Latin America, those years saw the fall from power of a number of important authoritarian rulers—Perón, Odría, Pérez-Jiménez, Rojas Pinilla, Batista, and Trujillo—producing an apparent "twilight of the tyrants" in the region.[8] In 1961 there was only one government in Latin America that had come to power through a military coup.[9] This was also a period in which many colonies in other parts of the world, particularly Africa, were achieving political independence and appeared to be establishing democratic governments, further adding to the impression that there was a trend toward democracy in the Third World.

This image of political change has been profoundly shaken by the events of the later 1960s and 1970s. These years have brought a new political reality to Latin America and to other Third World areas in which the predominance of democratically elected governments has given way to a predominance of military governments and authoritarian rule. Brazil, Peru, Chile, Bolivia, and Panama are among the most important and visible of the Latin American military regimes; the military or military leaders rule in a number of other countries; and Argentina and Uruguay have recently experienced a "militarization" of civilian rule. In addition, the two nonmilitary regimes with the longest records of stable, effective rule—those of Mexico and Cuba—owe their success in considerable measure to the successful establishment of one-party or one-party-dominant rule. Perhaps most embarrassing of all, the countries of Latin America that are the most socially and economically modern are now those in which this authoritarian rule is the most comprehensive and the most coercive.

Consequently, for Latin America as for other Third World regions, the earlier hypotheses that predicted democratization in the context of economic and social modernization have in substantial measure been discredited. However, this has not led to the abandonment of the search for systematic linkages between modernization and political change. Rather, it has encouraged scholars to look for different kinds of linkages.

Authoritarian Modernization

One of the most important sources of the new hypotheses about modernization and political change is to be found in the growing literature on authoritarian patterns of modernization.[10] Many of the arguments that have emerged from this literature can be organized around the idea of a "corporativist-authoritarian" developmental path, which is being followed by many Latin American countries, as opposed to the "pluralist-democratic" path that has been followed in certain other regions, particularly in the most advanced countries of Europe and North America.[11] In both types of countries, social mobilization, economic growth, and the structural differentiation of society create the potential basis for broader and more meaningful mass political participation and for a more pluralistic form of politics. However, this potential tends to be realized to a substantially greater degree in the democratic countries than in the authoritarian countries.

This difference appears to be due in part to the fact that the particular types of economic and social transformations that occur in the societies following the authoritarian path produce political groups that are often less capable of leading effective mass political participation.[12] In addition, the deliberate limitation of political pluralism by the state in these societies also plays a crucial role. This limitation of pluralism may be defined as the use of state resources to inhibit the emergence of autonomous political groups and to control or channel their political demand making. The state is thus not just a passive actor, but an active shaper of elite-mass, state-society relations.

Many of the most important developmental transitions that occur in authoritarian settings involve changes in the extent to which pluralism is limited and in the methods through which this is accomplished.[13] The exploration of these changes thus provides a useful focus for research on the linkages between modernization and political change. This focus coincides with that of the analytic tradition which has grown out of the pioneering work of Juan J. Linz, who has proposed that differences in the limitation of pluralism may be treated as an important dimension along which distinct subtypes of authoritarian rule may be arrayed.[14] The limitation of pluralism by the state is by no means an exclusive feature of authoritarian systems, and is obviously present to some degree in every political system. However, it is a particularly salient feature of authoritarian systems and appears to offer a useful focus for exploring the dynamics of authoritarian rule.

Within this framework of analyzing evolving patterns of limitation of pluralism, a series of themes will be emphasized. The first involves the question of the kinds of modernizing transitions that are most crucial in producing new approaches to limiting pluralism. Partly because many of the best-known studies of authoritarian modernization in Latin America have focused on such advanced nations as Argentina and Brazil, there has been a substantial emphasis in this literature on the causal importance of transitions that occur at relatively high levels of modernization. Attention has focused particularly on the political concomitants and consequences of industrialization based on import substitution and on the consequences of the apparent "exhaustion" of the initial "easy" phases of import substitution.[15] A supplementary perspective which has usefully focused attention on relatively high levels of modernization has been that which emphasizes the causal importance of the absolute, rather than the per capita, size of the modern sector in each nation.[16] This has permitted an invaluable conceptual regrouping of countries that places such important cases as Brazil more clearly among the highly modernized countries and provides the basis for a more adequate explanation of its political evolution.

At the same time that the causal importance of the transitions associated with the higher levels of modernization deserves close attention, transitions that occur at lower levels of modernization also merit attention, both because the more advanced transitions are not yet relevant for some of the less modernized countries and because crucial formative experiences that occur at low levels of modernization may have an abiding impact on national political life. It is this second consideration that is particularly relevant to the present analysis. Though import-substituting industrialization forms an important part of the overall context of economic growth in which settlement policy has evolved in Peru, it will be shown that some of the crucial modernizing transitions that have had the greatest long-term impact on settlement policy occurred many decades ago, long before the onset of any serious degree of import substitution.

The feature of the early pattern of modernization of Peru that is crucial for present purposes involves the distinction posed by Cardoso and Faletto concerning whether the export-led growth which occurred in many Latin American countries around the turn of the century was concentrated in isolated enclaves of economic modernity such as mines and highly mechanized plantations.[17] In contrast to the relatively marginal role of enclaves in such nations as Brazil and Argentina, this was the dominant pattern in Peru. As has been argued by diTella in his "theory of the first impact of economic growth"[18] and as will be shown later in this chapter with reference to Peru, this pattern of growth, though in one sense isolated within the national society, can produce patterns of economic, social, and political transformation which have over many decades a dramatic impact on the evolution of national political regimes and on the types of authoritarian rule that emerge. The political consequences of these transformations in Peru will be a principal concern of the analysis presented in the coming chapters.

A second theme that is of central importance to this analysis involves the fact that the relationship between economic and social modernization and changing approaches to the limitation of pluralism is not direct, but rather is mediated through a series of intervening variables. The process of modernization produces new economic and political groups. These groups interact in severe political crises, or "hegemonic" crises, in which the control of previously dominant groups is undermined by fundamental transformations in economic and social structure, by the mobilization of formerly passive political sectors, or by economic crisis.[19] These political crises are resolved through a reordering of the dominant political coalition on the basis of a new combination of economic and political interests and on the basis of the emergence of new tactics for incorporating or excluding the participation of newly mobilized groups according to their place within or outside the dominant coalition. These evolving coalitional patterns are crucial determinants of the approach to limiting pluralism that emerges out of each crisis.[20]

Third, with the evolution of different approaches to limiting pluralism, there appears to be a tendency toward a stronger assertion of authoritarian control over political life, particularly in the Latin American context.[21] Though the degree of control is by no means homogeneous across class lines[22] and though there may be important reversals in this tendency, the pattern of a stronger assertion of authoritarian rule at higher levels of modernization appears to be an important feature of contemporary Latin America. As the successive stages of settlement policy are examined, one of the questions to be raised by this study concerns whether this tendency toward a stronger assertion of authoritarian control does in fact emerge.

Finally, in connection with this stronger assertion of authoritarian control, there appears to be a greater degree of differentiation of political interests and a greater degree of autonomy of the state itself within the coalitional patterns that appear at higher levels of modernization.[23] The control and penetration of certain sectors of society by the state—particularly the working class—enhances its freedom of action and autonomy in a number of areas of policy making. The state thus becomes more than just a channel for expressing the interests of the dominant economic and social groups in the society; it becomes a separate actor with its own interests. An important early statement regarding this tendency appeared in Karl Marx's famous analysis of the growing autonomy of the state in France under Napoleon III, and this phenomenon is sometimes referred to as Bonapartism.[24] This pattern of growing autonomy may not accurately characterize all areas of policy making and may in some circumstances be reversible.[25] Nonetheless, it does appear to be an important tendency in authoritarian systems. The present study provides an opportunity to explore this tendency within the context of a particular area of policy change.

The analysis of the relationship between modernization in Peru and the evolving approaches to the limitation of pluralism which have been reflected in settlement policy will devote particular attention to these interrelated themes: the identification of the particular modernizing changes that have been crucial for policy change; the emergence of new political groups, political crises, and new dominant political coalitions; the tendency toward a more decisive assertion of authoritarian control over political life; and the tendency toward a greater differentiation of the political sphere and a growing autonomy of the state itself.

Economic and Social Modernization in Peru

Because a central concern of this study is to analyze the types of policy change that have been associated with the economic and social modernization that has occurred in a particular authoritarian setting, Peru, it is appropriate to introduce the most salient characteristics of that setting and of the type of modernization it has experienced.

There would be little disagreement regarding the characterization of the Peruvian political system as authoritarian. Recent Peruvian history has seen several important periods of military rule during which a central concern of the state has been to place substantial limitations on political expression.[26] The term "segmentary incorporation" has been used to describe a tactic that is common in Peru of giving substantial state aid to the most organized groups within an emerging social sector in a way that causes these groups to be more interested in seeking further benefits for themselves than in broadening and strengthening the power of the entire social sector.[27] Major policy innovations, such as an important early phase in the expansion of social security, have frequently been introduced in order to undermine radical political movements.[28] These tactics of preemption and control are unquestionably used in democratic systems as well. However, in a country such as Peru, they appear to be more pervasive and more comprehensive. In contrast to democratic countries, they are frequently applied by military governments which exercise far more complete political control than is found under the civilian regimes typical of democratic countries.

Peru has unquestionably gone through periods that are, at least superficially, democratic. Of the four policy periods considered in this study, both the liberal period (1956–60) and the period of party politics (1961–68) were characterized by a substantial degree of pluralism and of free competition among political parties. It will be shown that this more competitive pattern had important consequences for settlement policy. Overall, however, Peru has been a more predominantly authoritarian than democratic country, and the limitation of pluralism is correspondingly a central theme of settlement policy.

With regard to the patterns of economic and social modernization that have appeared in this authoritarian setting, it has already been emphasized that the pattern of growth of primary product exports that emerged in Peru around the turn of the century is of particular relevance for the present analysis. The pattern of urban growth that has occurred in this century is also of particular importance.

The Export Sector, the Apra Party, and Traditional Agriculture

The origin of many of the forces of change that are examined in this research is to be found in the rising importance in the late nineteenth and early twentieth century of the export of primary products from Peru —most importantly sugar and cotton from the coast and minerals from various regions of the country, particularly the central highlands. This development is crucial to the present analysis for two reasons.

First, the pattern of growth followed by the export sector produced the Apra party,[29] which has played a crucial role in shaping settlement policy in all of the periods considered in this study. The emergence of the export sector was based on a high degree of concentration of economic power in rural enclaves of economic growth. These new centers of economic power displaced important elements of the provincial urban middle class. The concentration of landownership also undermined previously existing patterns of small-scale agricultural production, producing a "proletarianization" of small-scale landowners, who in many cases became wage laborers in the new large enterprises. The combination of this economic and social displacement and the formation of a rural proletariat in the new enclaves of agricultural and mining activity created the conditions that led to the emergence of the Apra party, a coalition of this rural proletariat and the displaced middle class. Though there were relatively high levels of mechanization and hence, in a sense, of modernization within these enclaves, these developments occurred in the context of a relatively low overall level of modernization of Peruvian society, producing what might be viewed as a "premature" appearance of this new political party. Apra emerged as the principal force for radical change within the conservative context of Peruvian society.

Apart from the patterns of economic and social dislocation that *produced* Apra, it appears that the enclaves represent an ecological setting that is particularly conducive to *sustaining* a political movement such as Apra. DiTella has argued that in these "isolated mass" situations, "social mobility is low, and there is a common identification of the workers of the area against the 'rest of society,' perceived as distant and hostile. The labour market is often unstable, and this has a particularly strong effect owing to the absence of alternative sources of employment in the area. Group or community solidarity fuses with union solidarity, giving rise to a pattern of sharp social antagonisms. . . . The emotional charge that permeates [conflict] can be particularly strong in such cases."[30] This ecological setting appears to have been a crucial factor in sustaining Apra through many decades of repression.

Apra has, in turn, had a major impact on the evolution of settlement policy, in Peru, as will be shown in detail in the coming chapters. The political crises produced by this premature emergence of Apra and by subsequent attempts to incorporate Apra into the Peruvian political system have been one of the principal forces that have shaped settlement policy.

The second important consequence of the growth of the export economy from the perspective of this analysis was that it weakened the relative position of the traditional agricultural elite of the highlands, whose latifundia had generally been oriented toward local, or at most regional, markets. The elite of the export sector displaced this traditional elite as the dominant element in the Peruvian oligarchy.[31] In some parts of the highlands, the appearance of export-oriented mining and large-scale, highly efficient cattle raising which was linked to the development of large-scale mines became a stimulus for economic and social change which helped to erode the traditional agricultural order and, in some instances, drew the most able members of the traditional elite into these more modern enterprises, further weakening the traditional structure of control.[32] The declining proportion of national income produced by traditional agriculture also contributed to its declining political power. It has been estimated that by 1966 the value of the agricultural products of the traditional latifundia was as low as 5 to 10 percent of total agricultural production, not including the consumption of the Indians on the haciendas.[33]

The traditional elite's loss of dominance within the oligarchy was not in itself a fatal blow to its power. Its position depended in part on its control of local government in the highlands, which it was allowed to maintain in exchange for delivering votes in presidential elections.[34] However, in addition to these changes in the position of the traditional elite, other forces of change had begun by the early 1950s to affect traditional agriculture. Rapid population growth resulted in the fractionalization of landholdings, a worsening of the man-land ratio, and a decline in the standard of living.[35] Discontent was stimulated by the rise of new political parties, by rising levels of education, and by the spread of antioligarchic ideologies, in which the Apra party played a large role.[36]

Rural Change and Urbanization

These transformations in rural society have been a principal cause of another kind of social change that has played a central role in the development of squatter settlements in Peru—urbanization. In a setting of rural change such as this, three of the most important alternative sources of improvement in the life of the peasants are government-administered agrarian reform, land seizures and peasant movements, and out-migration. In highland Peru, the last of these three served until the early 1960s as one of the most important means through which the plight of the peasants was eased. Indeed, on the basis of research on other national contexts, it may be hypothesized that urbanization served as a temporary substitute for the other two.[37]

Analyses of migration patterns in Peru support this hypothesis that out-migration has functioned as a safety valve in rural areas. Principal causes of migration have included population growth, low productivity of agriculture, a declining standard of living, lack of opportunities for improving agricultural methods, and lack of alternative opportunities for employment.[38] For the peasants who stay in rural areas, out-migration improves the man-land ratio, increases agricultural production per capita, and improves living standards.[39] For those who leave the land, migration serves as a means of fulfilling economic and educational aspirations and achieving social mobility.[40] It has also been argued that the younger, more able, more educated portion of the population, which is most likely to migrate, is also more likely to become involved in peasant movements, suggesting another reason why there may be an inverse relationship between migration and pressure for political change in rural areas.[41]

While cityward migration thus appeared temporarily to protect the position of the oligarchy of the highlands, it also had important implications for other sectors of Peruvian society because of its consequences for the demographic and political importance of urban areas. The population of Lima—the focus of this study—rose from 3.9 percent of the national total in 1908 to 8.4 percent in 1940, 17.0 percent in 1961, and 24.2 percent in 1972. The proportion of the national electorate located in the Department of Lima showed a similarly spectacular increase, rising from 9.7 percent in 1919 to 28.2 percent in 1931 and 41.7 percent in 1961.[42]

This new urban population has formed an important part of the base of reformist political movements in Peru, including not only the Apra party, in spite of its rural origin, but also other reformist parties such as Acción Popular and the Christian Democratic party. The growing power of urban-based political groups in Peru represented a threat to the position of important sectors of society, in particular the export oligarchy.[43] This conflict between the export sector and new political movements based in urban areas is, of course, common in Latin American countries. It commonly crystallizes with the formation of the populist coalitions that make the break with the export sector by introducing basic changes in trade policy, enlarging the role of the state sector, and supporting industrialization.[44] It appears that the failure of Apra to hold power and bring similar transformations was due in part to the limited development of the urban political sector in Peru in comparison with a number of larger, more modernized Latin American countries.[45] However, the rising power of new urban groups—particularly mass-based political parties—was a continuing threat to the export sector. The steps that leaders of this sector have taken to protect themselves from this threat have been of great importance for settlement policy.

Peruvian Politics as a Living Museum

These processes of change in Peru—the growth of export agriculture; the "premature" rise of Apra; the declining power of the traditional highland elite; urbanization and the resulting growth of urban political sectors; and the growing divergence of interests among the traditional oligarchy, the export oligarchy, and urban-based sectors oriented toward fundamental reform—form the background of the present analysis of public policy toward squatter settlements. These processes of change have brought to power within a relatively short period a series of political groups representing extremely diverse class and political interests. The effect has been to create what Charles W. Anderson has described for

Latin America more generally as a "living museum" in which "democratic movements, devoted to the constitutional and welfare-state ideals of the mid–twentieth century, stand side by side with a traditional and virtually semifeudal landed aristocracy."[46] Peruvian politics appears to be a living museum not only because of the juxtaposition of a great diversity of political groups, but also because of the appearance within a relatively short period of a wide variety of alternative development strategies, alternative conceptions of the appropriate form of elite-mass relations, and hence of alternative policies toward squatter settlements. There has been a "telescoping" or a collapsing of stages in the development not only of political groups, but also of alternative policies. This juxtaposition of diverse groups and policies within a short period of time not only provides a convenient basis for comparative analysis, but has itself become a factor in influencing political change.

This research is concerned with examining the ways in which a sequence of different groups represented in this living museum of Peruvian politics has shaped settlement policy. The analysis focuses on four periods between 1948 and 1975: (1) the military government of Odría (1948 to 1956), the only government among those considered which had important ties to the traditional elite of the highlands, whose power antedated that of the export elite; (2) the first four and a half years of the second government of Prado (1956 to 1960), whose power was linked to the export oligarchy and to urban commercial interests; (3) a period (1961–68) in which settlement policy was dominated by the mass-based political parties whose power was, in important ways, created by the rise of the export economy; and (4) the period of military rule from 1968 to 1975 in which the reformist policies of the military have been in substantial measure a product of the crises produced by the political stalemate among the different groups that had influenced settlement policy in the previous periods. It will be shown that in each of these periods, the dominant political group has shaped settlement policy to fit its overall strategy of rural and urban development and its particular conception of the appropriate form of mass political participation and of the appropriate role of the state in society.

Conclusion

In the context of profound economic and social transformations that have emerged in Peru in the twentieth century, a number of processes of political change have occurred which have had a crucial impact on public policy toward the squatter settlements of Lima (see Figure 1). New eco-

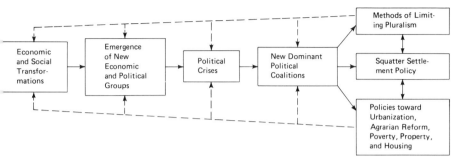

Figure 1. Modernization and Policy Change

nomic and political groups have appeared that have interacted in a series of political crises. These crises have in turn produced new dominant political coalitions that have come to shape settlement policy.

The choices that have been made regarding settlement policy have, in an important sense, been a product of these underlying processes of change. At the same time, settlement policy has been deliberately used to influence the future direction of these processes of change. This has been the case in part because of the degree to which settlement policy is linked to a series of other policies that are perceived as having an important impact on the direction of social, economic, and political change in Peru. These interrelated policies, which are discussed in detail in Chapter II, include policy toward urbanization, agrarian reform, poverty, property, and housing. In addition, and most importantly from the perspective of this analysis, they include the differing approaches to limiting political pluralism that have been adopted in each period. The purpose of this analysis is to explore the way in which these interrelated areas of policy have evolved in Peru and thereby to contribute to the understanding of the changing subtypes of authoritarian rule that have appeared in this particular context of economic and social modernization.

Issues of Settlement Policy
in Lima

The evolution of settlement policy in Lima has involved a complex set of issues concerning the settlements themselves and the relation between settlement policy and a series of other problems and issues: urbanization, housing, poverty, property, and the tactics used by successive governments for incorporating the political participation of the poor. In order to interpret adequately the broad relationship between modernization and this area of policy change in Peru, it is useful to have some understanding of these basic issues of settlement policy. This chapter presents a brief overview of the characteristics of settlements, emphasizing the most important policy issues that arise in connection with settlement development. It then explores the ways in which settlements and settlement policy are related to the other issue areas, focusing particularly on the trade-offs among the alternative goals which may be pursued through settlement policy.

Definitions and Labels

The expression *squatter settlement* is used in this book to refer to residential communities, formed by low-income families, in which the houses are constructed in large measure by the residents and which are generally, but not exclusively, formed illegally. The usual requirement of illegality has been loosened in this definition because, as will be shown, the extensive covert and sometimes overt state support for settlement formation makes the question of illegality rather complex. Some of the settlements that have received this support were actually formed legally, but have been treated in every other way like other settlements. Hence it seemed desirable to include them in the definition.

The present use of the term *squatter settlement* corresponds fairly closely to that of the current term for settlements in Peru, "young town" (*pueblo joven*).[1] Prior to 1968, the most commonly used term was the somewhat pejorative expression *barriada*, meaning roughly "little neighborhood." Other terms have included "lower class *barriada*" (*barriada popular*), "clandestine housing development" (*urbanización clandestina*), "clandestine neighborhood" (*barriada clandestina*), "floating neighborhood" (*barrio flotante*), "town in formation" (*pueblo en formación*), "marginal neighborhood" (*barrio marginal*), and "marginalized neighborhood" (*barrio marginalizado*). Expressions such as "social cancer" (*cáncer social*), "social aberration" (*aberración social*), and "belt of misery" (*cinturón de miseria*) have also been used to refer to the settlements.[2] These different terms for settlements have had considerable importance as political symbols, and at three points in the evolution of settlement policy a less pejorative name has been introduced to dramatize the shift in policy.

The Growth of Settlements in Lima

Lima offers an unusually favorable geographic and climatic setting for settlement formation. Because of the mild winters and the virtual absence of rain on the Peruvian coast, the minimal straw houses that first appear when settlements form are far more adequate than they would be in a less favorable climate. The absence of rain also simplifies drainage problems in these communities and eliminates the danger common in other areas of Latin America that settlements may be washed down hillsides in heavy rains. Finally, the fact that much of Lima is surrounded by unused desert land increases the opportunities for the formation of new settlements.

The appearance of settlements in Lima has been accompanied by a pattern of urban growth in which the city is constantly catching up with and surrounding settlements that are initially formed at the periphery of the city. Hence, at the same time that there are vast areas of newer settlements at the edge of Lima, there are also substantial areas of settlements that have long since been surrounded by the city. Many of the first settlements were formed in the area of the central market at a time when it was still at the edge of the urbanized zone of Lima (see Figure 2). As the city grew, these settlements were surrounded by new commercial and residential areas. The next major area of settlement growth, along both sides of the Rimac River, was occupied in the late forties and early

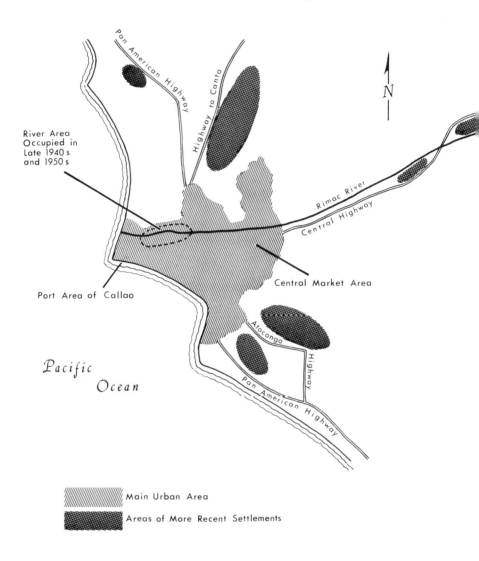

Figure 2. Squatter Settlements of Metropolitan Lima

fifties, again at the periphery of the city. By the late fifties, a substantial
proportion of this area, including the entire zone on the left bank of the
river, was also surrounded by commercial and industrial zones. Most of
the settlements that have formed more recently have appeared on desert
land even further from the center of the city, principally along five major
axes of highway transportation to the north, east, and south of Lima.

For most of the period considered in this study, there has always been more desert land available, located a bit further away along the principal axes of urban growth. However, a point has now been reached where the next available areas of vacant land are so far from the center of Lima that the earlier pattern of an apparently inexhaustible supply of unoccupied land has ended. As will be shown in Chapter VII, this had important implications for settlement policy in the period from 1968 to 1975.

The Physical Development of Settlements

Squatter settlements offer a desirable residential environment for the urban poor in large measure because of the pattern of development that they follow once they have been formed. To understand the importance of settlements for the poor of Lima, it is therefore essential to understand their pattern of physical development. Particular attention will be devoted to the policy issues raised by settlement development.

The initial formation of a settlement may occur in a variety of ways. In some cases, there is an organized invasion in which the land is seized at night, and the invaders must often fight off the police to retain possession. In many other cases, a group of families receives a formal or informal indication from the government that a particular tract of land may be occupied. In still other cases, the settlement forms through the gradual arrival of families and there is no well-defined starting point at which a large number of families occupy the land. These different types of formation are analyzed in detail in Chapter III.

Physical improvements in the settlement begin as soon as it is founded. Immediately after the occupation of the site, it is common for a truck to appear, selling the straw mats and poles that are used to construct the straw houses that represent the first stage of housing development in the settlement. Other trucks are likely to appear daily to sell water for household use. Though a water system is eventually installed in many settlements, these trucks commonly serve for many years as an expensive and inefficient means of providing water.

Depending on the type of area occupied, the growth of a settlement may continue for many years. However, this growth commonly has a natural limit, as when the settlement is located in a small valley, or between a road and a hill or ridge. This area is gradually filled by friends and relatives of the people who already live there and by others who hear that lots are available. The families who are already there generally try, often unsuccessfully, to regulate this growth, charging for new lots, attempting to maintain open areas for plazas, schools, and markets, and trying to prevent housing density from becoming too high.

Because of this pattern of gradual growth of settlements, a large proportion of the residents arrive well after the initial formation. In 38 of the 68 settlements on which there are appropriate data from the survey of settlement formation carried out by the author (referred to below as the survey of settlement formation),[3] nearly the entire population of the settlement arrived after the formation. In only 15 percent did those who arrived later represent less than a quarter of the population. The growth of a settlement generally continues over a fairly long period. In 25 percent of the cases, the growth continued for over ten years; another 19 percent of the settlements continued to grow for more than five years, and another 22 percent for more than three years. Only 16 percent completed their growth within one year.

Settlements generally have a dwellers' association that is the principal channel through which community development projects are organized. The officers of the association are usually elected annually by the residents. In the period immediately following the occupation of the site, the association is concerned with allocating and regulating lots and dealing with the police and any government representatives who may get involved in inspecting, aiding, or interfering with the new settlement. Later on, the association often initiates community improvement projects such as the construction of a school or community center or the building and leveling of streets. In many cases, the original association begins to fall apart once the problems associated with the formation of the settlement have been resolved, and a new group of individuals may later be brought together by their interest in some community project and reconstitute the association with the purpose of carrying out their plans.

Public policy has had an important impact on these associations. The government has, at various times, encouraged, regulated, and controlled the associations. During the 1960s, a decision to revitalize the local municipal districts in Peru shifted the focus of many development efforts in settlements to the municipal districts that included settlements, causing a decline of the importance of the local associations in many areas. However, their importance increased again after 1968 under the government of Velasco, which actively encouraged the associations.

The construction of houses in settlements proceeds along fairly well established lines. The first step after the construction of the initial straw hut is to build a brick wall that defines the perimeter of the lot. This is done as quickly as possible to avoid disputes concerning the size of the lot. Once this wall is completed, the construction of a brick house begins inside it, starting with a front room. The straw hut is commonly in the middle of the lot or at the back, and may continue to be used long after the construction of the brick house has begun. The purchase of an expensive wooden front door is an investment of major importance, since it provides security and represents a first, and highly visible, effort to beautify the house. Later, rooms are gradually added to the brick structure, a second story may be added, and a permanent roof constructed.

Though each family works primarily on the improvement of its own house, there is cooperation among neighbors, particularly in the more difficult stages of construction. There is also cooperation in community improvement projects, such as the building of schools, community centers, markets, the improvement of streets, and, in more advanced settlements, in the paving of streets, construction of sidewalks, and installation of water and sewage systems.

Squatter Settlements and Slums

A useful means of placing the advantages of settlements in perspective is to contrast the settlements with the slums of the center city, the principal alternative kind of housing that the poor of Lima can generally afford.[4] One of the basic differences involves a fundamental contrast in the security and stability of human life. Lima slums have been described as areas of great distrust and hostility among neighbors with a much weaker, less supportive associational life than settlements.[5] Considerable differences in crime rates have been reported by social scientists and are commonly referred to by social workers and others who have worked in both settlements and slums.[6] According to data drawn from the Survey of Lima carried out by the Survey Research Center of the Peruvian Ministry of Labor, settlements and slums differ in terms of a standard measure of "family stability": two-thirds again as many households in slums as opposed to settlements lack a male head of household—18 as opposed to 11 percent.[7]

The advantages of settlement life are reflected in the survey of settlement formation. Individuals who had been community leaders at the time of the formation of each settlement in the sample were asked to give the three principal reasons that led the families who founded the settlement to leave their earlier housing. Most of the families had come from slum housing in the center of Lima. Among the sixty-six leaders who came from slum areas for whom appropriate data were available, 58 percent mention high rent as a reason for leaving. Fifteen percent mention unemployment as a reason, meaning that they had to leave their rented housing for lack of income. Thirty-five percent mention the desire to own their own homes, and 20 percent mention crowding in previous housing.

Twenty-nine percent report that the group that formed the settlement was made up primarily of people who were being evicted from a particular area of slum housing, generally because it was being eradicated to make way for a highway, a public building, or a new housing development. An additional 6 percent indicate that the group was made up of people who were being evicted from two or more different areas of slum housing.

Settlements and slums also differ in the proportion of families who rent their dwellings. Five percent of the settlement respondents in the Survey of Lima, as opposed to 78 percent of the slum respondents, report that they are renters. It is likely that there is some underreporting of renting in settlements, since according to government regulations there is not supposed to be any renting in government-recognized settlements and sometimes people will not admit that they are renting. Nonetheless, it is clear that there is an overwhelming difference between settlements and slums in the proportion of people who rent their homes.

The combination of this difference in renting and the opportunities that exist in settlements for home improvement through self-help encourages the development of long-term commitments to improving one's home and community. This commitment is reflected in the Survey of Lima, in which 62 percent of the respondents in settlements, as opposed to 21 percent in slums, report that they plan some home improvements. The average amount that settlement residents intend to spend on these improvements is four and a half times as great as in slums.[8]

It appears that successful efforts at community improvements in settlements, once they have occurred, build expectations of future community improvements. In inner-city slums, where the opportunities for community improvement are much more limited, there is less likely to be a history of past community improvements that could form the basis for anticipating future improvements. This link between past and anticipated future improvements comes out clearly if one compares settlements that have varying rates of improvement. Among 82 respondents in the survey of settlement formation, there is a pronounced tendency for community leaders who reported higher levels of community improvement in the previous five years to anticipate more improvements in the coming five years.[9] Combining data from another Ministry of Labor survey with data on rates of community improvement collected in the survey of settlement formation, it appears that respondents who live in settlements with higher rates of community improvement have a greater tendency to like the area in which they live.[10]

A series of additional differences between settlements and slums emerges from the Survey of Lima suggesting that settlement residents are more satisfied with life in Lima and more fully integrated into it. A question about satisfaction among migrants reveals that settlement residents are more satisfied with Lima, as opposed to their home province, than residents of slums.[11] In spite of this, a larger percentage of settlement residents are able to identify community problems in the area in which they live.[12] The reason for this appears to be the link noted elsewhere between the capacity to solve problems and the tendency to be able to identify them: settlement residents were *also* more inclined to say that the problems should be solved by the residents of the community themselves.[13] Though most respondents were registered to vote and had voted in the previous election, there was a greater tendency among slum residents to fail to register or fail to vote.[14] Settlement residents likewise had higher levels of associational and party participation than slum residents.[15] Finally, settlement residents tended to score higher on an additive index that measured degree of orientation toward getting ahead within the norms of the established system.[16]

There is some indication that this difference between settlements and slums in satisfaction and integration into urban life depends in part on an ongoing pattern of community improvement in settlements. In those settlements that were not developing as quickly, levels of satisfaction were lower. Similarly, because settlement residents had become more sensitized to identifying problems, perhaps as a result of their greater ability to solve them, they may be particularly susceptible to frustration if their aspirations for problem solving are not realized. Thus it may be not the mere existence of settlements that is crucial, but rather the fact that they maintain a continuing pattern of community improvement. Though the findings regarding this complex issue of change over time are far from conclusive,[17] it is clear, as will be shown below, that in many periods the government has been concerned about this issue and has actively sought to encourage community improvements in settlements.

Factors Influencing the Development of Settlements

There is great variation within settlements, and between settlements, in the rate at which home and community improvements take place. Within a settlement, the amount of effort that a family is willing to expend on home improvement depends on such factors as the degree of security that it feels about the possession of the lot. If some of the lots in a settlement have been registered with the government housing agency, the residents of these lots feel more secure and are therefore more inclined to invest.

Families who live on lots that have not been registered, have poorly defined boundaries, or are in an area where there is a possibility that a road will be put through, are unlikely to invest in their houses.

The same factors help explain differences among settlements in the development of individual houses and community facilities. A settlement that has well-defined lots, has been promised land titles, or has received substantial government aid in a way that legitimates its existence, develops more quickly. A settlement that feels even a vague threat of eradication is unlikely to improve. In 1962, when a government housing agency classified settlements into six categories, one of which indicated that the settlement would eventually require eradication, the investment climate in the settlements in this last category worsened considerably. Most of these settlements were, in fact, never eradicated. Similarly, if the lots in a settlement are poorly laid out and there is a possibility that a government housing agency will eventually rearrange the houses in order to widen streets and regularize the size and shape of lots, it is unlikely that there will be much investment, since there is a chance that the houses will be torn down.

Other factors influence the development of settlements as well. Delgado has distinguished between internal settlements, which are initially formed near commercial or industrial areas or are surrounded by such areas as the city grows, and peripheral settlements, which are outside of the industrial and commercial zones of the city.[18] For a number of reasons, the peripheral settlements are more likely to develop than the internal settlements. One factor explaining this difference is the availability at the edge of many peripheral settlements of land to which relatives and friends of residents who come into the settlements as lodgers can move, thereby keeping the housing density at a lower level. Secondly, because of the accumulation of experience with settlements in Lima, and because of the influence of state housing agencies, settlements that have formed since the mid-fifties—generally peripheral—have tended to be laid out more carefully, with a regular arrangement of lots, wide streets and free areas for plazas, schools, and community centers. This makes them more pleasant places to live and makes it more likely that the residents will feel that home improvement is a good investment. Finally, the well-ordered lots and streets of the peripheral settlements were responsible for still another advantage. In the 1960s a government housing agency, operating with limited resources and anxious to produce the greatest possible impact with these resources, concentrated its aid programs in the peripheral settlements, whose problems were more readily soluble.

Among the factors that influence the rate of development of settlements, some are difficult to alter through public policy and others relatively easy. The age of a settlement and its location in an internal, as opposed to peripheral, area are obviously hard to change. Because settlement residents tenaciously resist eradication, it has been difficult to adopt any systematic policy of moving the residents of internal settlements to peripheral areas. Because of the high cost and high degree of resistance on the part of the residents to remodeling settlements by rearranging the basic grid of streets and lots, it has also been difficult to make fundamental improvements in settlements that were badly laid out at the time of their formation.

On the other hand, greater security can readily be provided by the state. Land titles, state investment in infrastructure, state assistance to community development projects, and other acts by the state that reflect its commitment to the settlements have a considerable impact on the residents' sense of security in the settlements and their willingness to invest and improve their homes and communities. The principal state efforts to aid settlements have therefore come in these areas.

Urbanization, Settlements, Housing, and Poverty

The appearance of squatter settlements in Peru, and in developing countries more generally, is closely linked to the process of rapid urbanization. On the one hand, urbanization is clearly a cause of settlement formation, and settlement policy serves as an inexpensive means of dealing with the pressures of housing shortages and urban poverty which accompany rapid urbanization. Settlement formation may thus help to explain why urbanization has not brought more disruption to Peruvian social and political life than it has. On the other hand, the use of aid to settlement formation and development as a means of dealing with these pressures may in turn encourage more urbanization. The following pages will explore these interrelations among urbanization, settlements, housing, and poverty.

Urbanization and Settlement Formation. The growth of settlements in Lima has occurred in the context of a massive increase in the city's population. The population of the metropolitan area increased from roughly 150,000 in 1908 to over 500,000 in 1940 and over 3.3 million by 1972. This represents an increase by a factor of more than twenty over the sixty-four-year period, with an increase of nearly 240 percent from 1908 to 1940 and of nearly 540 percent from 1940 to 1972. The growth of the settlement population has occurred primarily during the second of these two periods. Starting from a negligible level in 1940, it rose to over 300,000 by 1961, representing 20 percent of the metropolitan population, and over 800,000 by 1972, representing 25 percent of the metropolitan population.[19] Rapid growth has continued since 1972.

This pattern of urban growth and settlement growth is not atypical of Third World countries. Lima's rate of growth placed Peru tenth among the twenty countries conventionally defined as Latin America in the rate of growth of urban centers of 100,000 or more from 1950 to 1960, and fourth from the top for 1960 and 1970. Compared with other Third World regions, these urban growth rates placed Peru below Africa, but equal to or somewhat above most countries in Asia and the Middle East.[20] The proportion of Lima's population in settlements, though high, is likewise not unusual for Third World cities. The proportion of squatters in some cities is even higher: 30 percent in Cali, 33 percent in Karachi, 35 percent in Caracas, 45 percent in Ankara, and 50 percent in Maracaibo.[21]

The problems that rapid urban growth poses for city dwellers and for development planners are well known. In the context of rapid growth, major efforts are required merely to maintain previous levels of welfare in such areas as housing, employment, income, and health facilities. The widely held goal of increasing welfare is often unobtainable. However, it appears that in Lima the existence of settlements makes an important contribution toward achieving these goals.

Housing. The growth of settlements in Lima has helped to ease one of the major problems associated with rapid urban growth, the shortage of low-income housing. This shortage was first noted at least as early as 1922,[22] and the problem has received wide attention since that time. Various estimates have been made of the magnitude of the housing deficit, and the figures reported obviously vary greatly according to the criteria used to define inadequate housing and overcrowding. However, there is wide agreement that there is a serious housing shortage.[23]

For most of this century, government efforts to deal with the housing shortage have focused on the construction of housing by public and semipublic agencies. Examples of this approach may be found at least as early as 1918 in a law that authorized the state to build housing for public employees, and numerous laws have been passed since then that directly authorized the construction of housing projects or established semiautonomous agencies concerned with the construction of housing.[24] The Ministry of Development and Public Works has played a major role in housing projects. In addition, three semiautonomous state agencies have played a central role in housing construction in Lima: the National Housing Corporation, founded under Bustamante, and the Public Works Board of Callao and the National Health and Welfare Fund, both founded under Odría.[25] These three agencies had built over 10,000 dwelling units by the late 1950s, and thousands of other units had been built by other public and semipublic institutions.[26] By 1967 the total number of dwellings that had been built in greater Lima by public and semipublic agencies had reached 30,991.[27] If one assumes that there is an average of 5 residents per dwelling in these projects, this means that they have offered housing to roughly 150,000 people.

Other early measures dealing with the housing crisis included rent control and regulations intended to prevent the construction of substandard housing. Though intended to lower the cost of housing and improve housing conditions for the poor, these measures appear to have made conditions worse, rather than better. Rent control may have inhibited investment in housing, thereby worsening the shortage. Zoning requirements were so unrealistically strict that they could not be enforced and in fact gave the state less control over new housing developments than it might have had with more realistic standards. The construction of an important type of low-cost housing was banned, even though it was superior to many slum areas in which poor families lived.[28]

In comparison with the contribution of the state through the construction of public housing, squatter settlements have had a much larger impact in terms of easing the Lima housing shortage. There were over 500,000 residents in Lima settlements in 1967, the year of the population figure for public housing cited above.[29] As of that year, the contribution of settlements was thus well over three times as large. There has been a massive increase in the settlement population since then, making the contribution of public housing even smaller by comparison. Since the state has played an important, though often informal, role in encouraging settlement formation, the contribution of settlements to dealing with the housing shortage is in part a consequence of public policy. One of the important themes in the evolution of settlement policy in Lima is the gradual recognition of this contribution as a legitimate part of housing policy. The basic dilemma in this recognition involves a tension between the obvious merits of settlements as an extremely inexpensive kind of housing and the desire to apply traditional planners' standards to any housing with which national housing offices are associated.[30] In Peru, this conflict has increasingly been resolved in favor of a recognition of the merits of settlements.

Poverty. Apart from their contribution to easing the housing shortage, settlements also make a unique contribution to easing the problems of unemployment, underemployment, and low income among the urban poor. The free land and rent-free housing that the settlements provide represent a great benefit to low-income families, particularly in periods of unemployment, illness, and old age. Though low-income migrants lack the skills needed for many urban occupations, one skill they may bring with them is the ability to build their own houses. Settlements provide a setting in which this ability is relevant. In many settlements, the residents have space to keep a few animals—chickens, ducks, or guinea pigs— which are a source of food and also help a family to make it through periods of little or no income. Because settlements are commonly formed by groups of friends, relatives, and people from the same province, and because residents who arrive after the period of initial formation often come to join relatives or friends, the settlement resident tends to be surrounded by a network of friends and real and ritual kinsmen, forming an environment that lends itself to cooperation in community projects and to some degree in the construction of individual houses as well. These characteristics of settlements permit the development of an "urban subsistence economy"[31] in which it is much easier for poor families to survive on low incomes.

State assistance to settlements and settlement formation thus represents an inexpensive means of aiding the urban poor that is obviously attractive to governments that would like to deal with problems of poverty without any significant redistribution of income. As will be shown, this fact helps to answer the question of why there has been such a massive growth of settlements in Lima, given the oligarchic and authoritarian character of the Peruvian political system. The reason is that conservative governments have favored it. On the other hand, from the point of view of the political left, this type of aid to the urban poor has obvious drawbacks, since it eases the situation of the poor *without* the basic reforms the left favors. In the late 1950s, this issue of the way in which settlement policy and housing policy tend to obscure the more fundamental causes of poverty became an explicit theme in political debate in Peru.

Though in one sense the mere existence of settlements helps to ease the problem of poverty regardless of government policy, there has at the same time been notable variation in the approaches the government has taken to dealing with poverty through settlement policy. Two of these correspond to two of the principal types of development strategies that Anderson has identified in Latin America: the conventional approach, based on the elaboration of the existing private economic sector; and the democratic reform approach, based on meeting problems of development and poverty through an active state role.[32] During certain periods of settlement policy, there has been a major emphasis on encouraging the role of the private sector in assisting the development of the settlements. In other periods, massive state programs have played a more central role. A third approach, which falls before any of Anderson's development strategies in terms of its historical development, is the approach of traditional charity, which has also played a major role in settlement development. The circumstances of the appearance of these three alternative approaches to dealing with poverty through aid to settlements will be a central concern of the coming chapters.

Political Consequences of Urban Growth

Because settlements in Lima have eased the pressures of urban growth by helping to meet the problems of housing and poverty, they may thereby have reduced the extent to which urbanization has had disruptive social and political consequences in Peru. There is considerable ground for arguing that urbanization has a great disruptive potential, and the analysis of this potential has long been of concern to social scientists.[33] Research in this tradition has argued that cityward migration undermines traditional values and culture and leaves the individual dangerously isolated in a vast and anonymous city. This theme has been pursued by many authors, producing an "urban explosion" literature which has emphasized the dire political consequences of urban growth.[34]

As early as 1952, however, Oscar Lewis called attention to striking continuity in behavior between rural and urban populations.[35] He found that traditional behavior patterns and institutions of kinship and religion not only persisted, but in some instances were strengthened, by the move to the city. In later writing, he suggested that the constraints placed on human behavior by the culture of poverty help to account for this continuity.[36] The extremely short time perspective imposed on the urban poor by their daily struggle for survival produces a style of life little different from that which they knew prior to migration.

Since 1952, many other explanations have appeared of why urbanization does not necessarily bring abrupt social and political change.[37] First, it has been pointed out that migrants do not generally come directly from rural areas to large cities. Rather, families often follow a pattern of step migration, usually over several generations, in which members of the family move to progressively larger urban centers in a way that helps to prepare them gradually for urban life. Second, migrants tend to perceive cityward migration as a kind of upward mobility which has the effect of making them more conservative in the new urban environment. Third, the initial attempts to find housing and employment in the city commonly depend on contacts or opportunities offered by real and ritual kinsmen, so that far from isolating the individual from his extended family, migration may make him exceptionally dependent on it. Finally, the initial tasks of adaptation in the city absorb the migrant's attention, leaving little time to be concerned with broader political questions.

The opportunities for employment and housing offered by the city also have an important influence on the experience of migrants. In many cities, migrants find employment far more quickly than had been suspected, so that dissatisfaction with economic conditions is often less widespread than had been imagined.[38] The type of residential areas in which migrants find housing also has an important impact on their experience in cities. As was suggested above, the appearance of squatter settlements has been seen as an important factor in easing the transition to city life, serving as a social and political safety valve in contexts of rapid urban growth.

Another factor that influences the consequences of urbanization is the political and policy context in which it occurs.[39] This theme has been reflected in a considerable body of writing on Latin America. It has been suggested that the authoritarian character of the Brazilian and Mexican political systems have placed important limitations on the political expression of the urban masses in those countries.[40] With reference to Brazil, it has been argued that there is a strong historical continuity in the patterns of control of the squatter settlements (*favelas*).[41]

In Peru, it is clear that the massive growth of Lima has not brought drastic political change and that this outcome requires explanation. Urban growth has unquestionably been responsible for a greater centralization of Peruvian life in Lima and a correspondingly greater concentration of political life in the capital, but it has not had significantly disruptive consequences. Though the Apra party has been responsible for a considerable degree of political mobilization in urban areas, it was noted in Chapter I that the crucial events that were responsible for the formation of Apra occurred in rural, not urban, areas. There has been a massive growth of squatter settlements around Lima, but, as was noted above, this appears to be a constructive response to the problems of massive urban growth rather than the political threat it was once imagined to be. In Peru, as in Latin America more generally,[42] populist rulers have mobilized support among migrants in the cities. However, this mobilization has served far more to control the poor politically than to stimulate political demand making, and hardly involves the type of mass movement hinted at in predictions of urban upheavals. Peru has experienced a rural guerrilla movement, but not an urban guerrilla movement. The urban universities are major centers of radical politics, but this would appear to be due to their special characteristics as institutions within an urban society and not to the overall fact of urbanization.

The appearance of squatter settlements may help to account for this lack of urban political disruption. It appears that because settlements offer so many advantages to the urban poor—free land, rent-free housing, and opportunities for self-help in home construction and community development—the massive growth of settlements, and hence also public policy toward settlements, may have been a factor in limiting the political impact of rapid urban growth.

Settlement Formation as a Cause of Urbanization. In analyzing the connection between settlements and urbanization, it is important to emphasize that it is clearly a two-way relationship. On the one hand, settlement formation may occur in response to the pressures of housing and poverty associated with urban growth and may thereby serve as a means of averting the disruptive consequences of urbanization. On the other hand, there is good reason to believe that settlement formation encourages urbanization by offering inexpensive housing to cityward migrants.

New settlements are not initially formed by migrants who come directly from other areas of Peru, but typically by migrants who have first lived in slum areas of the central city, or in some cases in other settlements. Once a settlement has been formed, however, migrants often move there directly from other parts of the country. Hence, though many natives of Lima live in settlements, the adult population of settlements is made up predominantly of migrants. As of 1970, 75 percent of settlement residents over fifteen years of age were migrants.[43] Migrants have thus been the principal immediate beneficiaries of the development of settlements.

Apart from offering housing to migrants, settlements benefit them indirectly in other ways as well. Because settlements considerably reduce the shortage of low-cost housing and offer many other advantages to low-income families, the continuing growth of already established settlements has obviously made it easier for newly arrived migrants to make their way in the city. New migrants commonly stay with a friend or relative when they first arrive in the city. The likelihood that the friend or relative will have space to accommodate them is obviously increased because of the role played by settlements in reducing crowding in low-income housing. If the friend or relative lives in an uncrowded settlement at the periphery of the city, the new migrant will have a particularly easy time finding permanent housing, since it may be relatively easy to move to a vacant lot at the edge of the settlement.

The impact of the existence of settlements on migration patterns is not restricted to its influence on the experience of the migrant in the period immediately following migration. Though the pattern of moving back and forth from the city to the provincial place of origin is not as widespread in Peru as it is in Africa,[44] the decision to be a migrant to a large city is an ongoing choice in Lima as well. The fact that settlements considerably ease the life of the migrant population surely has a long-term effect on the decision to stay in Lima. Hence it appears that at the same time that settlement formation has in part been caused by rapid urban growth, it may itself encourage urban growth.[45]

Alternative Policies toward Urbanization. Because settlement formation may encourage further urbanization, there is a fundamental dilemma that policy makers must face in using settlement policy to deal with problems of urban growth. It may be argued that there are two types of policies for dealing with problems of urbanization. On the one hand, there are many ways of improving the lot of people who are in the cities—including welfare programs, public housing, efforts to increase urban employment, efforts to encourage private investment in low-income housing, and programs that encourage community development and self-help efforts among the urban poor.[46] These approaches all tend to encourage further urbanization.

On the other hand, many policies for dealing with problems of urbanization are intended to prevent it from occurring, reduce the extent to which it occurs, or influence the direction it takes. These include the formation of satellite cities near major urban centers; attempts to encourage the development of secondary cities; the strategy of "concentrated decentralization," which focuses on core regions and social development poles; land reform in areas of traditional, unproductive agriculture; programs to build major highways, which open up previously underpopulated regions; and colonization projects, which establish new cities or encourage agricultural development in previously undeveloped areas of the country.[47]

Any program that aids settlements or settlement formation obviously represents a policy of the first type, i.e., one that tends to encourage further urbanization. In the coming chapters, an important theme will be the trade-off between the desire to aid settlements and the desire to discourage migration to Lima. One of the factors that is most important in affecting the choice between these alternatives is the policy of each government toward agrarian reform. Chapter I suggested that there may be an inverse relation between urbanization and the need for agrarian reform. Policy makers in Peru appear to have been sensitive to this trade-off; there has been an inverse relationship between how willing they are to carry out agrarian reform and how concerned they are about the tendency for settlement formation to encourage further urbanization.

Property

The legal status of the land on which settlements form is another basic issue of settlement formation. Three types of landownership may be identified: public, in dispute, and private. Among 84 cases of formation or attempted formation on which detailed information was available, roughly 44 percent involved public land, 35 percent disputed land, and only 19 percent private land.[48] The surprisingly high proportion of cases involving disputed land results from the widespread ambiguity of landholding in the Lima area. This ambiguity results in part from a homesteading system that exists under Peruvian law allowing individuals to establish ownership of public land for agriculture or mining.[49] Individuals who claim to own land, or even plan to claim land, under this system may call the police if the land is occupied by squatters.

Another source of ambiguity concerning landownership is the tradition of constitutional provisions and laws that requires that land must be used in harmony with "social interest" and that unused land reverts to the state.[50] These notions concerning the nature of property are basic to the legal system of Latin America, having been an important means through which the Spanish Crown attempted to control the use of land in the colonial period, as well as an important aspect of land disputes and land reform in the modern period.[51] These legal provisions are the cause of many ambiguities of landownership in greater Lima and have also raised the expectation among would-be squatters that unused land really *ought* to be public. Though there has recently been an increased concern with these ambiguities of property law, the state has generally done little to resolve them. Not only has it neglected the possibilities for reform built into the legal system, but, since the colonial period, it has failed to use its powers even to maintain unambiguous records of landownership.[52]

Though these ambiguities of landholding and the failure to exercise more control over land use in greater Lima have clearly benefited low-income squatters, it must be emphasized that they have by no means been the only beneficiaries. Apart from settlement formation, many types of illegal, or at least legally ambiguous, appropriation of land may be found in greater Lima which have benefited the wealthy as well as the poor. One common type involves abuse of the system of homesteading referred to above. Under Peruvian law, land that is acquired under this system cannot be used for housing developments until twenty years have elapsed after the initial concession is granted.[53] Several famous cases of illegal use of land in Lima involve the violation of this provision. One of Peru's leading banking families established a large housing development to the east of Lima through such a violation. A nephew of President Odría also established a housing development on land to the south of Lima that he had acquired for agricultural purposes.

Other types of illegal use of land have occurred as well. The family of a past president of Peru came to have a major role in real estate development in Lima by illegally acquiring land that should have reverted to the state because its last owner had died without heirs. There are many cases in which haciendas in the vicinity of Lima were expanded by simply putting nearby public land under cultivation. In some cases in which landowners have protested the seizure by squatters of land that they claim to be their own, the land actually involved hillsides at the periphery of the city that, under Peruvian law, belong to the state.

Finally, settlement formation itself has benefited the wealthy as well as the poor. In over a quarter of the 60 settlements for which appropriate information was available, the initial formation of the settlement served to facilitate the eviction of residents of inner-city slums so as to make way for private or public urban development projects. The new settlement offered them alternative housing at a point when they were often resisting eviction. In this sense, settlement formation has helped to perform the "urban removal" function of much urban renewal in the United States.

Two other settlements were formed when an extended dispute over an eviction from an inner-city slum ended in a suspiciously timed fire that made it easier to force the families to leave.[54] Three additional settlements were formed by families who were being evicted from two or more different areas of inner-city slums. Three other settlements were formed following evictions of groups of families from rural areas. These were cases in which families who had been living on land that was part of a farm or quarry where they were working were evicted by the owner and forced to settle in a nearby area. In all of these cases it was obviously the interests of the owners that were immediately served by the formation of the settlement.

In two additional cases, the immediate beneficiaries were would-be owners who used squatter invasions to help establish their claims to particular pieces of land. In one case, a woman who wished to claim some unused land to the north of Lima gave "permission" to a group of families to occupy part of the land and thereby turned these families into militant partisans of the idea that she was the owner. This maneuver put on her side a force of readily mobilizable poor families that she could use to protect her claim if the state or another private claimant tried to have her removed from the land. In the other case, a municipal government controlled by a political party that was in opposition to the national government wished to get control of some land that was claimed by a powerful landowning family. By arranging an invasion on part of the land, it succeeded in getting control of the area in which it was interested. Scattered evidence suggests there have been additional cases in which invasions were used to establish claims to land.

Altogether, out of the 60 cases on which appropriate information was available, nearly 50 percent in some way benefited public or private urban development or real estate interests. The ambiguities of landownership in Lima have unquestionably served the wealthy as well as the poor.

These findings concerning patterns of land use provide further insights into why settlement formation has been permitted. It has been permitted because it is part of a larger game in which the wealthy and the powerful have benefited greatly. The findings also provide insights into policy change. This game has been possible only because of the large amount of unused land that has been available around Lima, and because the lack of respect for property law that is part of the game was not a matter of concern to the government. During the twenty-five-year period covered by this study, the terms of this game have changed markedly because of changes in the availability of land noted above and because of an increased concern on the part of the government with respect for law.

The issue of what is to be done about the legal status of land *after* a settlement has been formed is another important aspect of settlement policy. If land titles are granted, the resulting sense of security is likely to produce higher levels of self-help and investment in the settlements. In the absence of titles, there is likely to be a greater sense of insecurity on the part of settlement residents and of concern with whether the state will continue to tolerate the occupation of the land to which the residents do not have title. This insecurity may seriously limit the willingness of settlement residents to invest resources in their community and thereby inhibit community development.

Strategies of Political Incorporation

A final issue that has been of great importance to settlement policy is the evolution of different strategies of incorporation of mass political participation that has occurred in Peru. Squatter settlements and public policy toward settlements have frequently been used as a means of linking the urban poor to the state in a way that is viewed as constructive, rather than disruptive, by the government in power. The characteristics of settlements lend themselves to a variety of different tactics for accomplishing this. On the one hand, the insecurity associated with not having land titles and fearing eradication, which was noted above as a negative feature of settlement policy, may also serve to create a relationship of dependence between the settlements and the state which discourages certain types of political behavior that the government might find disruptive. On the other hand, the opportunities for self-help offered by the settlements can serve to create a kind of autonomy and self-sufficiency in the settlements that make radical political alternatives irrelevant. Still another alternative lies in the local community organizations that exist in the settlements. If these organizations are captured and controlled by the state, it may permit a very complete penetration and control of the political life of the settlements. These alternative tactics of creating dependence, creating self-sufficiency, and penetrating and controlling the political life of the settlements have all been employed during the periods considered in this study. The pattern of evolution from one tactic to another and the reasons why particular governments have chosen one tactic over another will be a central concern of the analysis.

The links between the urban poor and the political system involve not only issues of political control, but also the ways in which political support is expressed. The organizational characteristics of settlements lend themselves particularly well to an important means of expressing political support—mass demonstrations. An important issue of settlement policy in all periods concerns the degree to which, and the means through which, this potential source of support is cultivated.

Conclusion

This chapter has provided a number of preliminary answers to the question of why settlements have been permitted to form in Lima. Their formation was permitted, in part, because it provided an inexpensive solution to the housing shortage and to the problem of poverty. Settlements also offer important opportunities for incorporating the urban poor into Peruvian political life in a way that is advantageous to the government.

At the same time, there are tensions and dilemmas associated with settlement policy. Dealing with problems of urban growth through the encouragement of settlements produces more urban growth. The use of settlements to ease the housing shortage requires the abandonment of traditional planners' standards about the minimum acceptable characteristics of residential neighborhoods. Permitting the widespread appropriation of land by squatters is perceived as being inconsistent with respect for property law. Finally, alternative strategies of incorporating settlement

residents politically, particularly the choice between encouraging dependence and encouraging autonomy, are in a sense mutually exclusive. A
central concern of this book is with exploring the alternative ways in
which these tensions have been resolved by different governments.

Government Support
for Settlement Formation

One of the most important aspects of government policy toward squatter settlements is policy toward settlement formation itself. This chapter presents an overview of government involvement in settlement formation in Lima. The focus is on the basic types of formation that have occurred; the relative importance of the government role in settlement formation; the ways in which the police have reacted to the formation of new settlements; variations in the police reaction according to the type of land that is occupied and the extent of government support for the settlement; and the major periods of evolution of government support for settlement formation. A concluding section attempts an overall characterization of policy toward settlement formation. The analysis, which is based on data through 1972, employs both a smaller sample of 84 settlements on which detailed information is available and a larger sample that includes an additional 52 settlements on which less detailed information was collected.

The method of selection of settlements for inclusion in the study deliberately overrepresented two types of settlements. Because a major purpose of the study is to analyze government support for settlement formation, cases of suspected government involvement were automatically included. Inferences from the sample to the universe must obviously be made with this bias in mind. In addition, larger settlements are more important because they offer opportunities to find new housing to many more people. Hence they were also overrepresented. Because of this emphasis on larger settlements, the smaller sample includes 81.7 percent of the total settlement population of Lima, even though it includes only 40.4 percent of the settlements. The larger sample includes 90.2 percent of the residents and 65.4 percent of the settlements. An extended discussion of the survey of settlement formation that was used to collect these data is presented in Appendix I.

Types of Formation

The three principal types of settlement formation in Lima have been invasions, gradual formation, and government authorization.

Invasions

One of the most widely held images regarding squatter settlements is that of the squatter invasion, in which poor families band together, seize unoccupied land at night, and fight off the police in order to escape the dismal conditions of inner-city slums. This image had contributed greatly to the argument that settlements represent a "threat to sovereignty" in the Third World.[1]

Invasions have played an important role in settlement formation in Lima and have received considerable attention in the literature on Lima settlements.[2] Some invasions involve relatively small groups of families who join together on an informal basis shortly before the occupation of the land. Others involve hundreds of families and are planned with great care. The leaders of these invasions often organize well before the invasion occurs and meet many times to recruit members, choose a site, and plan the occupation itself. In the most elaborately planned invasions there are systems of delegates who are responsible for recruiting members from given areas of the city and who are in charge of the families from their area when the land is occupied.

Gradual Formation

In cases of gradual formation, there is no well-defined moment at which a substantial group of families occupies the land.[3] This type of formation may occur in a semirural area where one or a few families are living in shacks on land that they are cultivating or quarrying and are joined over the years by other families who build houses nearby, producing a pattern of gradual growth of the community without any well-defined starting point. Cases of gradual formation have also occurred within the city in situations in which construction workers build temporary houses on vacant land near construction sites where they are working. Rather than leave when the construction is over, they stay on and are joined over the years by other families.

Government Authorization

The literature on Lima settlements has largely neglected government authorization as a type of formation, though instances of the involvement of political groups in the formation of settlements have been mentioned. Mangin, for instance, notes that in one period the government showed considerable leniency toward invasions,[4] and says that the support of a sympathetic political leader may be sought by the invasion group to provide protection from police intervention.[5] Turner describes a case in which a citywide settlement organization provided important support for an invasion, and Dietz refers to a case in which a government housing agency relocated families in a squatter settlement.[6]

These observations on the role of political groups represent a useful step toward suggesting the importance of political support for the formation of settlements. However, there has not previously been sufficient evidence about a large number of cases of settlement formation to assess either how important political support has been or the types of governments or groups that have most actively given it. According to the evidence from the survey of settlement formation conducted by the author, political support has in general taken the form of formal or informal government authorization, usually from the national government, although in a few cases municipal governments have been involved. Political parties operating independently of the government have also played a role in settlement formation.

In one type of government authorization, the formation of the settlement resembles the basic invasion pattern, except that there is an informal suggestion from a government official, often a representative of the president, that a particular piece of land is available for occupation and that the police will not interfere if it is occupied. This type of government involvement may be motivated by the desire to gain political support, but it is also used as a way of facilitating the eviction of tenants from inner-city slums in order to permit wealthy landowners or the government to develop the land for other purposes.

In other cases of government authorization there is a more formal, public approval of the occupation of the land, occasionally through a special decree or law. In such cases, the formation does not take the form of an invasion at night, and often government or army trucks carry the families to their new home sites, at times simply leaving them in the desert to build their new community. Such authorizations are usually accompanied by promises of title to the land, though until recently these have rarely been granted, and settlements formed with this type of authorization often end up being indistinguishable from those formed in other ways in terms of the legal status of the land. This type of government involvement occurs in a variety of situations. It may occur when a dispute over an eviction has become public and the government wishes to intervene dramatically to give the impression that it is concerned with the plight of the poor. In other cases, it may be used to aid families who have been left homeless by a flood, earthquake, or fire. Such authorizations have also been used systematically as a means of gaining political support from the poor.

The government has also intervened in many cases after the initial formation of the settlement in order to prevent the police from evicting invasion groups. Since these settlements begin as relatively spontaneous invasions, they will be treated for the moment as invasions and the importance of these postinvasion interventions will be examined later.

Relative Importance of the Three Types of Formation

An examination of the data on settlement formation suggests that of these basic types, that involving government authorization is far more important than has previously been recognized. In the larger sample of 136 settlements referred to earlier, the three basic types of formation are of approximately equal importance, with 30 percent of the cases involving government authorization, 37 percent invasions, and 30 percent gradual occupation (see Table 1). The remaining 4 settlements did not fall clearly into any of these categories.

Because settlements vary greatly in size, not only the number of settlements in each category but also the proportion of the settlement population that lives in each type of settlement must be considered. This reflects the importance of each type of formation in terms of the number of families to whom it has offered an opportunity to find better housing.[7] From this point of view, government authorization is by far the most important type of formation. Sixty-one percent of the residents of settlements in the larger sample live in settlements formed by government authorization, as opposed to 27 percent in those formed by invasion and 11 percent in those formed by gradual occupation.

Since the government role in settlement formation has involved not only outright authorization, but also intervention after the occupation of land in cases that were classified above as invasions, these figures underestimate the importance of the government role. The smaller sample of 84 cases on which there is more complete information may be used to examine the government involvement in greater detail.[8]

TABLE 1. Types of Settlement Formation as of 1972

Type of Formation	Larger Sample				Smaller Sample			
	Number of Settlements	Percent	Population	Percent	Number of Settlements	Percent	Population	Percent
Government Authorization	41	30.1	465,169	61.3	35	41.7	460,495	67.0
Invasion	50	36.8	205,762	27.1	37	44.0	177,539	25.8
Gradual Occupation	41	30.1	85,008	11.2	11	13.1	48,702	7.1
Other	4	2.9	3,079	0.4	1	1.2	580	0.1
TOTAL	136	99.9	759,018	100.0	84	100.0	687,316	100.0

Looking more closely at the cases of formation previously classified either as government authorizations or as invasions, the following types of political involvement in settlement formation may be distinguished: (1) informal intervention by some branch of the national executive before the invasion to encourage the formation of the invasion group and indicate that land is available; (2) public authorization by some branch of the national executive before the occupation of the land; (3) informal intervention by the national executive after the occupation of the land to limit police intervention; (4) involvement of a political party other than that of the president; (5) possible government involvement, but lack of full information; and (6) no apparent political involvement.

Among the cases in the smaller sample that were classified earlier as government authorizations, most involved either informal intervention by the government before the occupation of the land or public authorization before the occupation (see Table 2). In the remaining 4 cases, occupation was authorized by a nonpresidential political party. In these last 4, all in the 1960s, the settlements appeared in a municipal district that was controlled by a nonpresidential political party and thus involved authorization by a municipal government rather than the national government. Among the cases that were originally classified as invasions, 10 involve informal intervention by the government after the occupation of the land.

TABLE 2. Type of Settlement Formation by Role of Political Groups
(Government Authorizations and Invasions from Smaller Sample)

Role of Political Group	Type of Formation		
	Government Authorization	Invasion	Total
Informal government intervention prior to occupation of land	15	–	15
Public authorization prior to oc-cupation of land	16	–	16
Informal government intervention after occupation of land	–	10	10
Intervention by nonpresidential party	4	5	9
Possible government involvement, but ambiguity or insufficient information	–	7	7
No apparent political involvement	–	15	15
TOTAL	35	37	72

Five involve some role of a nonpresidential party, though in none of these cases could this be said to have been crucial in the formation of the settlement. Seven involve some evidence of a government role but not enough to permit assigning the cases to another category, and in 15 cases there is no evidence at all of government or party involvement.

One may assess the overall importance of government involvement by indicating the number of settlements in which the support of the government may be said to have been crucial. It was certainly crucial in outright cases of government authorization, and it may be argued that it is also crucial in the 10 instances of informal government intervention since, failing this intervention, the police would probably have evicted the invaders. In addition, we may somewhat arbitrarily say that in half of the cases of possible government involvement (rounded to 4 out of 7), the government role was crucial. This gives a total of 49 cases out of 72, or roughly two-thirds, in which the government role was crucial. Since this sample is biased toward cases of government involvement, this impressive figure is obviously too large. One would not wish to infer from it that the government role was crucial in two-thirds of all cases of settlement formation in Lima. However, we can come closer to estimating the overall proportion by adding the 6 cases of government authorization from the larger sample that were not included in the smaller sample (see Table 1). There are thus 55 cases out of 136, or 40 percent of the larger sample, in which the government role may be said to be crucial. If the total number of settlements in Lima is 208,[9] it may still be argued that the government role was crucial in the formation of more than a quarter of the settlements in Lima at the very *least*. This is obviously an overly modest estimate of the importance of the government role, since there are certainly additional cases of government involvement among the settlements not included in the sample, as well as in those on which there is less complete information. The real percentage is somewhat higher.

If the findings are presented in terms of the percentage of the residents who live in these settlements, the results are even more impressive. These 55 settlements have a population of 563,169, or two-thirds of the settlement population of Lima. Thus, at the very *least*, half a million people— that is, over a sixth of the total population of metropolitan Lima—live in settlements in whose formation the government played a crucial role.

Police Reaction and Ownership of Land

Another important aspect of government policy toward settlement formation is the reaction of the police to invasions. Under Peru's highly centralized police system, the national police force, the Guardia Civil, has the responsibility for dealing with invasions. The Guardia Civil is part of the Ministry of Interior, earlier called the Ministry of Government. Though the police are part of the national government, there is not necessarily perfect coordination between the police and the policy of the president or of government housing agencies. In fact, as will be shown in later chapters, there were two important periods in which the minister of interior independently established a special relationship with the settlements.

Police reaction to invasions has ranged from not appearing at all to the violent eviction of the invaders, with a variety of responses in between, including appearing at the invasion site but taking no action; attempting only to prevent the arrival of additional families who are not members of the original invading group, and hence limiting the size of the invasion; making a symbolic effort to evict the invaders, perhaps by knocking down a few of the huts, without seriously attempting an eviction; and seriously attempting to evict, but failing. Though it would seem surprising that the government would be unable to evict squatters if it wished to, in some instances the resistance of the invaders has been so tenacious that after an

initial attempt the government gives up. In other cases, political consider-
ations have led to an abandonment of the eviction after an initial
unsuccessful attempt.

The analysis of types of police reaction will be based on the 72 cases in
the smaller sample that involved invasions or government authorization,
plus 12 instances of prior invasions that occurred before the main
occupation of land that was subsequently occupied by a settlement
represented in this sample. All 12 of these resulted in evictions. The most
common police responses were at the two extremes: not appearing at all
(38 percent) and evicting the invaders (26 percent). The other 4 responses
each occurred with roughly equal frequency—approximately 10 percent
of the time.[10]

Apart from the relative importance of each type of reaction, the
circumstances under which each type tends to occur is also of great
interest. It may be hypothesized that the ownership of the land and the
type of political support enjoyed by the group that occupies the land will
influence the police reaction.

The ownership of the land on which settlements have formed was
classified into three types: public, in dispute, and private. Among the 72
cases of government authorization or invasion, 51 percent involved public
land, 28 percent disputed land, and 19 percent private land. Among the
cases of evictions that occurred on sites that were later occupied by
settlements, only 1 occurred on private land, and most were on disputed
land. These evictions thus did not occur on land that was unquestionably
public. Considering all 84 cases together, there was a clear tendency for
the police reaction to be mild when public land was involved and most
harsh when the land was private. The reaction when disputed land was
involved falls in between.[11]

The police reaction also depended on whether the group occupying the
land had political support. Prior government authorization guarantees
safety from eviction, and all but 1 of the 30 cases of serious attempts to
evict (with or without success) occurred in cases of invasions. However, it
is interesting that there were 2 symbolic attempts to evict and 1 serious
attempt to evict in cases of authorization.[12] One of these occurred in a
situation in which a government housing office authorized an occupation
but the municipal government in whose district the occupation occurred
tried to prevent it from taking place by sending the police. The municipal
government and the agency were associated with rival political parties.

Though prior government authorization generally makes eviction
unlikely, an examination of the more detailed breakdown of the role of
political groups in settlement formation suggests considerable variation in
the police role according to the type of political support the settlement

has. Public authorization before the occupation of the land is relatively certain to guarantee that the police will not come, but informal authorization is sometimes followed by vigorous police intervention—though never by an eviction. Informal intervention after the occupation is always directed at limiting a police intervention that has already begun, so that this informal intervention occurs only in cases in which the police have already appeared. There were no cases in which informal government intervention after the occupation of the land failed to prevent an eviction. All but 1 of the evictions involved settlements that had no political support, or were cases of ambiguous information.[13]

It thus appears that both landownership and political support affect the reaction of the police. Not surprisingly, these causes are strongly interrelated. Government-authorized settlements are predominantly (74 percent) on public land.[14] Because of this strong relationship between the government role and the type of land involved, it is difficult to be certain which is most important in influencing the police reaction. It appears that the relationships among these variables is quite complex, and the causal relationship in some cases may not even go in a consistent direction. For instance, whereas the legal status of the land is generally one of the factors that determines the police reaction, in one period the willingness of the government to evict invaders encouraged wealthy landowners to make a claim to land when it was invaded. Hence the anticipated police reaction influenced the legal status of the land.

Periods of Formation

Since the focus of the present study is on variations in settlement policy over time, the findings about the characteristics of settlement formation in Lima become particularly interesting when they are presented in terms of different historical periods. It must first be noted that settlement formation has tended to be concentrated in certain periods (see Table 3). In terms of the number of settlements formed, the first major period was that of Odría, with the second government of Prado also being one of major importance. In terms of present population, the first major period was again that of Odría, with the settlements formed during the first four years of the Velasco period also having a very large population. By 1975 the population of the settlements formed under Velasco was substantially larger than that of the settlements formed in any of the earlier periods.

With regard to the different types of formation, there is a clear evolution in the pattern of government involvement. The period through the "1945 ambiguous" category was predominantly one of gradual

TABLE 3. Number and Population of Settlements Formed
under Each President, as of 1972
(Larger Sample)

President	Number of Cases	Percent	Population	Percent
Pre–Sánchez Cerro (1900–30)	2	1.5	2,712	0.4
Sánchez Cerro (1930–31, 1931–33)	3	2.2	12,975	1.7
Benavides (1933–39)	8	5.9	18,888	2.5
Prado (1939–45)	8	5.9	6,930	0.9
1945–ambiguous[a]	5	3.7	24,335	3.2
Bustamante (1945–48)	16	11.8	38,545	5.1
Odría (1948–56)	30	22.1	203,877	26.9
1956–ambiguous[a]	2	1.5	11,890	1.6
Prado (1956–62)	30	22.1	93,249	12.3
1962–ambiguous[a]	2	1.5	22,377	2.9
Pérez Godoy (1962–63)	2	1.5	1,737	0.2
Lindley (1963)	3	2.2	11,046	1.5
Belaúnde (1963–68)	15	11.0	93,407	12.3
Velasco (1968–72 only)	10	7.4	217,050	28.6
TOTAL	136	100.3	759,018	100.1

[a]One major source of data for the larger sample indicated the year, but not the month, of formation. Hence, for a few settlements, it was not possible to be certain whether they were formed under the outgoing or the incoming president.

formation, with 17 of the 26 settlements being cases of gradual formation. Five of the 9 remaining settlements were invasions, and there were just 2 authorizations. Under Bustamante, there was a sharp increase in the proportion of invasions, and in 5 of these invasions the government intervened after the occupation of the land to prevent police eviction. This trend toward government involvement became even more pronounced under Odría, when there were only 3 cases of formation in the smaller sample in which there is no evidence of some government role. The other two main periods of settlement formation—the second government of Prado and the government of Belaúnde—likewise show a variety of kinds of government involvement and few cases in which political groups had no role at all.[15]

Finally, there has been substantial variation over time in the severity of police reactions to invasions. Among the periods for which sufficient information is available (since 1945), the highest proportion of evictions—70 percent—is under Velasco, with no evictions under Bustamante (see Table 4). With regard to serious attempts to evict which did not result in evictions, it is noteworthy that there are 4 of these under Bustamante. It will be shown in the next chapter that these cases represent an important phase in the early history of government involvement in settlement formation.

Characterizing Government Policy

The data thus suggest that government support for settlement formation has been extensive and that public policy has therefore played a major role in settlement formation in Lima. Before proceeding with the more detailed analysis of policy change in the coming chapters, it is appropriate at this point to assess the type of public policy that has been involved.

Because the appropriation of land by the poor has been a central feature of settlement formation, this area of policy might appear to involve

TABLE 4. Police Reaction to Settlement Formation
(Government Authorizations and Invasions in Smaller Sample
Plus 12 Cases of Prior Invasions)[a]

President	Percent Evictions	Percent Evictions Plus Serious Attempts to Evict	Total
Bustamante	0	67	6
Odría	10	15	20
Prado	26	37	19
Military Junta (1962–63)	43	57	7
Belaúnde	22	22	18
Velasco	70	70	10
		TOTAL	80

[a]Four cases are missing from this table because of the exclusion of 3 cases of formation and 1 prior invasion which occurred prior to 1945. There were too few cases under any one president in these earlier periods to permit any meaningful comparison.

the redistribution of land from the state or, in a few cases, from wealthy landowners to the poor. From this perspective, the basic issue of settlement formation and settlement policy would seem to be the willingness of the state to let this redistribution occur. This perspective has, in effect, been adopted by Mangin and Delgado, the only authors who have thus far attempted to characterize government policy toward settlement formation in Peru. They have both used the term *liberal** to describe the political climate of the Belaúnde period which made it possible for settlement formation to occur relatively freely in the 1960s in Peru.[16] The implied interpretation would seem to be that liberal governments are more concerned with the benefits that the poor derive from settlement formation than with a rigid interpretation of property law. Talton Ray has approached settlement formation in Venezuela in a similar fashion, describing as "permissive" and "lenient" the attitudes toward the poor of the reformist Acción Democrática governments of 1945 and 1959 that led them to tolerate extensive settlement formation.[17] By contrast, he says that the Venezuelan military ruler Pérez Jiménez (1952 to 1958), who was hardly a liberal, was "dedicated to maintaining order. . . . and staunchly defended government and private property. . . ."[18]

On the basis of the present analysis, it is clear that this characterization based on the idea of liberality does not fit the case of Peru. The implicit frame of comparison on which Mangin and Delgado base their observation appears to involve the contrast between the higher proportion of evictions and attempted evictions under the second Prado presidency and the military government of 1962–63 and the lower proportion under Belaúnde. It is certainly correct in terms of overall policy that Belaúnde's government was the most liberal of these three, in the sense in which Mangin and Delgado are using the term. Yet the causes of the differences in settlement policy among these three governments are complex, as will be shown later, and are not really related to their liberality. The explanation of liberality fits other periods even less well. A comparison of the degree of repression of organized labor under Odría and Prado's second presidency suggests that Prado is the more liberal,[19] yet in terms of settlement policy Odría was obviously more permissive.

The basic problem with this conception of settlement policy as redistributing land from the state and the wealthy to the poor is that it is based on an excessively narrow definition of the policy. It is unlikely that

---

*They mean liberal in the sense in which one speaks of a welfare-oriented Democrat in the United States as being liberal. This differs from the usage in this book, where the term is used to refer to the laissez-faire ideology and economic policies that are associated with classical liberalism.

a wealthy person would want a lot in a squatter settlement,[20] so that as long as the policy is defined only as a policy toward settlement formation, it will inevitably involve only the transfer of land to the poor. However, policy toward settlement formation is a part of a broader policy toward land use in the greater Lima area. Chapter II suggested that there has been a long tradition in Lima of appropriation of land by a wide variety of individuals and groups, both wealthy and poor. It is only when this broader context of policy toward control of land is considered that it will be possible to assess meaningfully the political relationships that are involved in settlement policy.

Placing settlement formation in this broader context of appropriation of land makes it easier to identify the type of political game that is involved. In view of the fact that police evictions of squatters have occasionally occurred and that a number of settlements were formed on disputed land, one could get the impression that this was an area of policy characterized by a high level of conflict. However, the cases of disputed land and the evictions were, in fact, a by-product of the informality of the system of land distribution and the ambiguities of the unresolved claims for land concessions. This assertion would appear to be supported by the fact that during the Belaúnde period, when, as will be shown, government support for settlement formation became more formalized, the proportion of evictions was lower. The periodic occurrence of conflict and coercion in connection with settlement formation was the result of the low degree of formality in government land policy generally, and of the failure of the government to regulate land use effectively in greater Lima.

Far from being highly coercive, the system was, in a sense, infinitely generous. A group of squatters that was evicted could usually find another site to invade, and a wealthy claimant, if he lost one area of land to a squatter invasion, could make another claim elsewhere. An important factor that contributed to the flexibility and informality of this area of policy was the divisibility of the good that was being acquired, that is to say, the divisibility of land. Land can be subdivided, and land in one area can be substituted for land in another area, in contrast to certain other goods, such as clean air, which all of the residents of a given community either possess or do not possess together. If land was not available in one area, the needs of a group of squatters or a wealthy landowner could be satisfied with land in another area. In some instances, the need was satisfied by granting land in several different places, as when an evicted invasion group was relocated by the government on land by the edge of two or more different settlements that had already been established.

This combination of informality and divisibility is illustrated by an extraordinary case involving a government authorization of a settlement to facilitate an eviction from an inner-city slum area. After being persuaded to leave their former homes, the evicted families were loaded onto government trucks and taken to an area of vacant land to the north of Lima. The residents of a nearby settlement objected to having them located on that particular site, and the government trucks moved further up the road, seeking another location. Once again, the residents of a nearby settlement objected, and finally the trucks left the families still further up the road in an area where settlements had not yet begun to form. In this case and many others, settlement policy was generally able to operate as if there were always more land available up the road, both for the poor and for the wealthy.

Though the public policies that have these characteristics of informality and divisibility might almost seem to be nonpolicies because of the extent to which they operate by default, they actually correspond to an important type of policy that has received considerable attention in research on the United States. Theodore J. Lowi has called these policies "distributive," a term first coined to describe nineteenth-century land policies in the United States.[21] Lowi argues that

> distributive policies are characterized by the ease with which they can be disaggregated and dispensed unit by small unit, each unit more or less in isolation from other units and from any general rule. . . . These are policies that are virtually not policies at all but are highly individualized decisions that only by accumulation can be called a policy. . . . In many instances of distributive policy, the deprived cannot as a class be identified, because the most influential among them can be accommodated by further disaggregation of the stakes.[22]

These sentences could have been written to summarize the characteristics of the government policy toward land use in Lima.

The striking thing about the policy being considered here is the fact that it is the *control of land* that is being treated distributively. Though the United States has certainly had land policies, such as the Homestead Act, that were distributive, the maintenance of a well-defined system of property has also required the use of the coercive and regulative powers of the state—aspects of state activity that Lowi identifies with a type of policy which is clearly distinct from distributive and which he calls "regulative."[23] The Latin American tradition is quite distinct. Latin American property law has been characterized by a tradition of forceful rhetoric in favor of the use of land in the interest of society. In practice, however, the state has often been unsuccessful in regulating the use of land, either to achieve general social goals or even for the purpose of defining unambiguously who owns what property. The informality and relatively low level of coercion in the Peruvian government's policy toward settlement formation are thus aspects of the general way in which property has been treated politically in Latin America.

Conclusion

This chapter has suggested that the Peruvian government has been extensively involved in supporting settlement formation in Lima. There was little government involvement prior to 1945, with a major increase occurring in the Bustamante period, followed by substantial government involvement under most governments since that time. It was argued that it is misleading to explain this involvement in terms of the idea that the liberality of certain governments has permitted the redistribution of land to the poor. Rather, settlement policy must be seen as part of a broader policy from which the wealthy as well as the poor have benefited—both because real estate interests have benefited directly from settlement formation and because the wealthy themselves have taken advantage of the ambiguous definition of land ownership by appropriating land for their own use.

Apart from the fact that a variety of individuals and groups, both wealthy and poor, have benefited from the relaxed enforcement of property law in greater Lima, there are other reasons as well for arguing that the poor have not been the only beneficiaries of settlement formation. It was suggested in Chapter I that settlement policy has many purposes apart from simply aiding settlement residents. In addition to representing an important aspect of policy toward urban poverty and urban housing shortages—matters that directly affect the welfare of the urban poor—settlement policy is also linked to broader policies concerning patterns of rural and urban development and patterns of control of property, as well as to the tactics adopted by each successive government for incorporating the political participation of the urban poor. As will be shown in the coming chapters, choices regarding these policies, and hence regarding settlements, have involved an elaborate interplay of differing class and political interests in which there have been many beneficiaries from settlement formation and settlement policy in addition to the settlement residents.

IV

Paternalism and Informality:
Settlement Policy under Odría

The first period of settlement policy to be examined in detail is the period of paternalism and informality that corresponds to the populist-military government of Odría, who held power from 1948 to 1956. The central factor responsible for the coup that brought Odría to power was a severe crisis of mass political participation that Peru experienced in the middle to late 1940s. The purpose of this chapter is to show how settlement policy was used to help resolve this crisis and to try to identify the origins of the particular approach to elite-mass relations that Odría applied to the settlements. In attempting to explain settlement policy in the Odría period, the analysis will also provide an explanation of one of the most important findings of the previous chapter: the sharp increase after 1945 in the rate of settlement formation and the extent of government involvement in settlement formation.[1]

The Political Crisis of the 1940s

A central feature of Peruvian politics in the mid-1940s was the attempt to bring the Apra party back into the established political system following a period in which it had been illegal.[2] As indicated in Chapter I, this party grew out of the economic and social displacement caused by the emergence of the export enclaves starting at the beginning of the twentieth century and was made up of a coalition of middle-class and working-class elements. Its early history was characterized by a radical reform program—given the Peruvian context—and by considerable

55

political violence. The response to Apra of the dominant groups in the Peruvian political system has alternated between attempts to bring the party into the established electoral system and outlawing and repressing it.

The period considered here involves one of these attempts to reincorporate the party into the electoral system. Apra had been legalized in time to enter the 1945 elections as part of the National Democratic Front. This coalition won the election for its candidate, Bustamante y Rivero, who was not an Aprista, and Apra won a majority in the Congress.[3]

With the reemergence of Apra, this was a period of intense political mobilization. Apra worked vigorously to build its party base, and once in the Congress used public money for projects that helped to strengthen party organization. This was also a period of growth of the labor unions which formed a major part of Apra's base of support, and there was a sharp increase in the number of unions recognized by the government.[4] Finally, it was a period of considerable political violence, much of which appeared to be attributable to Apra.[5] This violence included the assassination in January of 1947 of Francisco Graña Garland, editor of the newspaper *La Prensa*, which had been conducting a vigorous campaign against Apra.[6]

In an important sense, the game of squatters and oligarchs in Peru begins with the killing of Graña, since this incident was the immediate cause of the entry into the struggle with Apra of two leaders who would later play a major role in shaping policy toward squatter settlements: Pedro Beltrán, a leading oligarch, and General Manuel Odría, a future president of Peru. These two men were responsible for introducing two contending approaches to squatter settlements in Lima that over the following twenty-five years would periodically reappear in settlement policy: the liberal approach and the paternalistic approach. Beltrán had been the Peruvian ambassador to the United States at the beginning of the Bustamante government, but with the killing of Graña he returned to Peru to take over the editorship of *La Prensa* and to continue Graña's campaign against Apra.[7] For Odría, the assassination marked the beginning of his political career, since it was responsible for his appointment by Bustamante to the position of Minister of Government. As head of this ministry, Odría was in charge of police and had full responsibility for investigating the assassination and other violence that was occurring.[8]

Odría became the center of anti-Apra sentiment in the cabinet, a role that was relatively easy for a military officer to assume in light of the long tradition of enmity between the armed forces and Apra.[9] It is hard to imagine that Odría was not already thinking of a military coup by this time. He unquestionably knew that Perón had just come to power in Argentina after a period in which he held a cabinet post. He must also have been aware of Perón's successful effort to mobilize support in the Argentine working class from his position as Minister of Labor. In the Peruvian context, it was clear that given the massive popular support that Apra enjoyed and the legitimacy that it had achieved through its electoral success, any military government would do well to have its own base of popular support to legitimate its rule. It was in this setting that Odría, while still Minister of Government, first became involved in settlement formation.

Evidence presented in the previous chapter suggested that the period between 1945 and 1948 saw a sudden increase in squatter invasions. Fragments of information about these invasions indicate that individuals from political parties were involved, including the Communist party and perhaps also Apra. Though the police initially made vigorous attempts to evict the invaders, there is clear evidence that from his position as Minister of Government, Odría halted these evictions in at least three cases and permitted the invaders to stay on the land. This helps to account for the large number of unsuccessful attempts to evict during the Bustamante period, which was noted in the last chapter. These interventions represented a first step toward the major government role in settlement formation that emerged during the Odría presidency.

In early October of 1948 a faction of Apra attempted a military coup, which was quickly suppressed.[10] President Bustamante outlawed Apra, and three weeks later Odría toppled the coalition government with a coup of his own, initially enjoying the strong support of the powerful export sector of the Peruvian oligarchy as he assumed the presidency. This group wished to end the period of political instability and crisis that Peru was experiencing and also desired to end certain economic policies that had been pursued under Bustamante and that were unfavorable to its interests.[11] The export oligarchy provided important financial support for the coup,[12] seeking to use the military as its political instrument in an attempt to restore order in Peru.[13] Other interests played a part in the coup as well. There had been important reductions in the military budgets between 1945 and 1948, as well as other measures that the military found threatening,[14] and this coup, like many others in Latin America, was used to strengthen the position of the military within the government. Finally, Odría's personal ambition was also a central factor.[15] The government that emerged was not one of the military as an institution—as the post-1968 regime would be—but rather a government run on a very personalistic basis by Odría himself.

Odría's Presidency

Once established in office, Odría sought to destroy Apra's power and the union and party groups that it had formed. A Law of Internal Security, passed in 1949 and retained throughout the Odría period, eliminated most judicial restraints that might have hindered Odría's campaign against Apra.[16] Large numbers of party members were arrested, others went into exile, and unions and union federations linked to Apra were destroyed or taken over by leaders sympathetic to Odría.[17] However, Odría's campaign against Apra was based not only on repression, but also on a strong appeal to the lower classes in which he tried to offer an alternative to the kind of popular mobilization that Apra was promoting. It has been argued that Odría "was antiunion but not antiworker. While on one hand he gave employers what amounted to complete liberty to destroy the unions in their shops, he would give startling wage and social benefits to the workers. He decreed, for example, seven blanket wage increases while in power. . . . [Odría left] power with many people convinced that he had done more for the worker than anyone in the history of Peru. Odría's labor policy was, in an elephantine manner, paternalistic."[18]

Odría's aid for the poor took many other forms as well. He sponsored a number of public housing projects that provided new homes for low-income families[19] and these projects and other programs of public works in Lima brought a boom to the construction industry and a sharp rise in working-class employment.[20] In his effort to establish a more paternalistic relationship between state and the poorer classes in Lima, Odría placed heavy emphasis on charity and gifts to the poor. In this way he sought to provide an alternative to the political arrangement that Apra had been trying to promote in which the benefits from the government came in response to mobilization and articulation of the interests of the lower classes.

Odría's wife, María Delgado de Odría, in imitation of Eva Perón,[21] wife of the populist president of Argentina, played an important role in this show of paternalism. She made numerous charitable visits to the poor which were extensively publicized by pictures on the front page of the government newspaper, *La Nación*. The María Delgado de Odría Center of Social Assistance, formed in imitation of a similar organization of Eva Perón's, was a principal channel for her charitable activities.[22] The tone of María's relationship with the poor is reflected in a book-length apology for the Odría government published in 1953.[23] The summary of the chapter dealing with her activities included the following subheadings:

The Christianizing mission of the first lady of Peru; Her untiring fight for the well being of the poor; How she won the love of the poor; . . . The human transcendence of her work. The leadership of an admirable woman; . . . Torrent of love; The language of the people.[24]

The chapter included a number of personal stories of people whom she helped.

Odría and Squatter Settlements

Among the most important aspects of Odría's effort to reestablish a more paternalistic kind of politics in Peru was his extensive promotion of the formation of squatter settlements. As was shown in the last chapter, this was a period of active government involvement in settlement formation. Among 18 settlements in the smaller sample formed in this period, there were 4 cases of public authorization before occupation of the land, 6 cases of informal authorization before the occupation, 2 cases of informal intervention after the occupation, and 2 more with some suggestion of government involvement but incomplete information. One invasion was sponsored by the opposition to Odría, and there were only 3 cases in which there was no apparent political involvement.

Odría and his wife were actively and publicly identified with the settlements, and many of María's charitable activities focused on settlements. Settlements whose formation Odría aided were named after Odría, Odría's wife, Odría's home province, and the wife of a close associate of Odría's. The names included Villa María del Triunfo (Village of María the Triumphant) and Villa María del Perpetuo Socorro (Village of María of Everlasting Aid). One settlement was formed on Odría's birthday, and another on María's birthday.

At the same time that Odría aided settlements and settlement formation, he also used settlements as a base of political support. This exchange relationship is illustrated most clearly in the close ties which he developed with the largest and most important settlement whose formation he sponsored, the Twenty-seventh of October, named after the date of his coup. In 1951 a special law was passed that created a new political district for this settlement and granted to the dwellers' association of the settlement the power to enroll members who would settle in the district.[25] The association, called the Asociación de Padres de Familia Veinte-Siete de Octubre (literally, the Association of Fathers of Families of the Twenty-seventh of October),[26] was run by close associates of Odría, and in order to move to the Twenty-seventh of October one had to join the association. Though initially anyone could join, except for known Apristas, toward the end of Odría's term of office, when he was considering running for president again in 1956, the members of the association were required to become members of Odría's party. Through this organizational tie, and through frequent personal visits, Odría and his wife developed a particularly close identification with the Twenty-seventh of October. By 1956, nine thousand members of the association had received land in the Twenty-seventh of October, and thirty-one thousand more were still waiting for their lots.[27] Though a settlement of nine thousand residents is small in comparison with those of the 1970s, it was then the largest settlement in Lima.[28]

This dwellers' association played an active role in demonstrations of political support for the president. The headquarters of the association was decorated with large pictures of Odría and his wife, as well as of Perón and his wife.[29] Members of the association, and of other settlements as well, were periodically marched to the central plaza of Lima in demonstrations of support for Odría on occasions such as the anniversary of the coup, Odría's birthday, and his wife's birthday. The association also took out full-page newspaper ads to commemorate these occasions.[30] These demonstrations were even carried on after Odría left office. For instance, in 1961 a demonstration of settlement residents greeted Odría upon his return from a long absence from the country.[31]

Odría's Strategy of Incorporation

Through devices such as these—offering land to the poor to form settlements, charity in the settlements, the use of names associated with Odría, and demonstrations in the central plaza—Odría sought to build the idea that the poor enjoyed a special relationship with him. This was part of Odría's attempt to establish a dependent, paternalistic relationship between the president and the poor and to undermine the type of political relationship that Apra had been promoting, in which forceful political demand making was carried out by groups organized to a considerable degree along class lines in parties and unions. A crucial aspect of this paternalistic relationship was, of course, the fact that in exchange for aid to the settlements, Odría received extensive popular support which helped to legitimate his rule.

In spite of the extensive and public involvement of the Odría government in promoting settlement formation, it is striking that there is no evidence that Odría ever granted land titles to the settlement residents.

When viewed in terms of Odría's concern with reestablishing a paternalistic relationship between the government and the popular classes, this failure is quite understandable. If the squatters are simply located on public land, their security of tenure on that land appears to depend on the willingness of the state, and particularly the president, to let them stay there. If they receive title, their security of tenure has a formal legal basis that is independent of the good will of the president. The failure to give land titles thus reinforced the idea that the squatters were dependent on having a special connection with the president of Peru. Serious discussion of granting titles did not begin until the later 1950s, and the effective granting of titles did not begin until the late 1960s, when political pressure from the mayor of a squatter settlement district finally forced the adoption of laws that established simple and effective means of granting title.

This type of dependent political relationship is, of course, in no way unique to Peru. It clearly corresponds to what Powell has described as clientelism. Powell has written that the "contract between patron and client . . . is a private, unwritten, informal agreement, and highly personalistic in content. There is no public scrutiny in the terms of such agreements. . . . This stands in sharp contrast to the relationship . . . in modern systems of political transactions. In essence, the patron-client pattern occurs in the realm of private accountability, the modern pattern in the realm of public accountability.[32] In the clientelist relationship, the lack of public accountability obviously works to the disadvantage of the client, because of "the degree of power asymmetry between superior and subordinate. Superiors in a clientele system are relatively free to behave in an arbitrary and highly personalistic manner in dealing with their subordinates. Subordinates in a clientele system have relatively little recourse in such a situation."[33] It was precisely this type of hierarchical relationship that Odría appeared to be promoting through his policy toward the settlements.

Apart from the question of informality, another way in which Odría's policies tended to increase the dependence of the poor on the government can be seen in Odría's sponsorship of certain types of political groups. Though Odría attempted to control political mobilization by destroying the strong party organization and aggressive labor unions that Apra had been promoting, he by no means tried to eliminate all political groups. Indeed, through his promotion of settlements, Odría encouraged the formation of the dwellers' associations that typically appear when a settlement is formed. These associations played an important role in Odría's relation to the settlements, for they formed the organizational basis for the numerous demonstrations in the central plaza and later for a political party through which Odría hoped to perpetuate himself in power. In a sense, these community associations did "mobilize" people to "participate" in mass demonstrations. However, this mobilization and participation served to express political support that was unrelated to demand making and was therefore quite distinct from the Apra movement.

In general, these settlement associations have not tended to make demands on the political system. They exist largely for the purpose of carrying out community projects and for cooperating with any state or private aid programs that are available, often changing their leadership at the beginning of the term of a new national president to maximize such cooperation. In promoting the formation of settlements and settlement associations, Odría was thus creating a new world of benign associational linkages for the poor which offered an important alternative to the forms of political organization that Apra had been promoting.

Because Odría's approach to settlements, based on paternalism and informality, was so clearly directed against Apra, it would seem fair to characterize it as part of the overall strategy for limiting political pluralism at this particular stage in the evolution of Peruvian politics. Since the methods of limiting pluralism have been identified as an essential dimension for distinguishing different subtypes of authoritarian rule, it may be argued that this stage of paternalism and informality does, indeed, reflect one stage in the evolution of authoritarian rule in Peru.

How does one explain the selection of this particular approach—that of paternalism and informality—to linking the poor to the state? On the one hand, it would seem logical that the granting of land titles would not begin to occur until a later stage in the evolution of settlement policy. Odría was receiving the political support that he desired, and he appeared to have a coherent strategy for shaping elite-mass relations. There would thus not appear to be any urgent reason for pursuing any approach other than informality and paternalism.

However, it is tempting to try to identify the models of elite-mass relations available in Peruvian society from which he might have drawn his approach to the settlements. There is a striking parallel between certain features of the organization of the haciendas of traditional agriculture in the highlands of Peru and the nature of Odría's relationship with the squatter settlements. Many haciendas were literally feudal, in the sense that an exchange relationship existed between lord and peasant in which labor was exchanged for the use, but not the ownership, of land. In the capital, Odría offered the use, but not the ownership, of land to settlement residents in exchange for political support.

The sector of the elite that had played a central role in bringing Odría to power was, of course, the export sector, and not the traditional elite of the highlands. The traditional elite obviously did not dictate the adoption of this particular type of policy. Yet certain important links between Odría and this sector of the elite should be noted. Odría was from a relatively traditional area of the central highlands and was the son of the manager of an hacienda.[34] In addition, particularly after his break with the export sector part way through his government (see Chapter V), the traditional elite of the highlands was among Odría's most important political allies.[35] Though the evidence does not suggest a direct causal connection between these facts about Odría and the form of settlement policy, there is a striking congruence.

Urbanization and Public Policy

Odría's policies also had important implications for cityward migration. It has already been suggested in Chapter II that settlement formation encourages migration to the capital and makes it easier for migrants to stay in Lima once they have arrived. Odría's extensive support of settlement formation would therefore appear to have encouraged urbanization. Other policies of Odría had this effect as well. The heavy concentration of public works spending in the capital[36] greatly increased working-class employment in Lima, and it has been shown with reference to Colombia that migratory movements are highly sensitive to employment opportunities.[37] Odría's large-scale programs of aid to the urban poor in Lima must also have encouraged migration to the capital. Taken together, these policies virtually constitute what may be called a "strategy of deliberate urbanization."[38]

This implicit policy toward urbanization is clearly consistent with the interests of one of the important social sectors that supported Odría, the traditional elite of the highlands. It was suggested earlier that urbanization may serve as an alternative to rural social and political change and that in Peru, out-migration appears to have played an important part in postponing the collapse of the rural social order of the highlands. Though no evidence is available suggesting that there was a conscious choice to encourage urbanization as a means of preserving the traditional rural order, it does appear that these policies were congruent with the needs of the traditional oligarchy.

Conclusion

Under Odría, squatter settlements came to have an important place in Peruvian politics. Odría showed that the government could actively support settlement formation as an inexpensive means of giving aid to the poor, as a means of gaining political support, and as a means of encouraging a very different political relationship between the urban poor and the state than that which had been promoted by Apra. In place of the pattern of class politics based on demand making through mobilization from below, Odría sought to promote an authoritarian pattern of informal, paternalistic linkages that tended to obscure, rather than intensify, class identification. In this sense, settlement policy was part of an overall strategy for limiting pluralism and reflected one aspect of a distinct subtype of authoritarian rule.

The Odría period also had an important impact on the kinds of political games that would be played in relation to the settlements in later years and on who would play those games. Invasion leaders who had worked for Odría had an important role in other invasions in the later 1950s. One high military officer who was closely associated with Odría's government and the son of another officer who was a member of Odría's cabinet would later attempt to build their own base of political support in the settlements. A future president and an important political leader who aspired to the presidency would develop a close political identification with a major settlement, just as Odría had done with the Twenty-seventh of October. Finally, the Twenty-seventh of October continued for many years to be of great political importance. For instance, the politician referred to above who led the campaign in the later 1960s to demand a simple and effective procedure for granting land titles was the mayor of this settlement.* Odría had created a new urban political sector, one that future political leaders could ignore only at great cost in terms of loss of political support—and perhaps also of political control.

Indeed, borrowing a phrase proposed by Albert Hirschman, it may be argued that Odría had set in motion a "sorcerer's apprentice dynamic" in which the initial offering of moderate benefits stimulated an ever greater demand to supply further benefits.[39] Not only had the expectation been raised in the minds of politicians and potential squatters that many additional new settlements could be formed, but the residents of the already established settlements also became a force to reckon with. Once

---

*At the beginning of the Prado period in 1956, in order to dissociate themselves from Odría, the leaders of the dwellers' association of this settlement changed its name to Urbanización Perú. The name of the municipal district was changed to San Martín de Porras.

the initial enthusiasm of founding the new community had worn off, what expectations would be raised regarding ways in which the state should aid the further development of the already established settlements? If extensive state aid were promised but not delivered, what kinds of pressures in favor of more effective or comprehensive assistance would arise? As will be seen in the coming chapters—particularly with reference to the issue of the granting of land titles—the issue of settlements in Lima, once politicized by Odría, followed a certain inner logic of its own in which each new stage of state commitment to the settlements in turn seemed to push policy makers toward even greater commitments. A central issue of settlement policy would be whether political leaders would respond to the temptation to broaden their commitments to settlements—as occurred in the period of party politics—or whether they would attempt to reduce these commitments—as occurred in the liberal period and in the period since 1968.

Autonomy and Self-Help: The Liberal
Approach to Settlement Policy

The second principal approach to settlement policy is the liberal approach,* emphasizing self-help and political autonomy among the settlement residents, as opposed to the dependency that was promoted in the Odría period. The liberal approach emerged out of the conflict between Odría and elements of the export and urban commercial elites. Correspondingly, this approach reflected many of the basic orientations and biases that members of these elites typically bring to policy making. In order to understand settlement policy in this second period, it is therefore appropriate to begin by summarizing the overall approach to public policy that has been supported by these elites.

In Peru, as in other Latin American countries, the export sector has traditionally been associated with liberal, laissez-faire policies. This sector has generally supported free trade and private enterprise and has opposed high taxes, large government programs, and a large role for the state in the economy. In contrast to the elite of traditional agriculture, whose power was based on semifeudal patterns of control of land, and in contrast to the political left, it is a staunch advocate of the protection of private property within a capitalist framework. In terms of development strategy, the export sector supports what has been described as the extreme laissez-faire variant of conventional development policy based on the encouragement of the expansion of the modern private sector of the economy and the assumption that the growth of this sector will eventually trickle down to the rest of the society.[1] Leaders of this sector tend to be, at

---

*In this sense, the term *liberal* is used to refer to the laissez-faire ideology and economic policies associated with classical liberalism.

the very least, ambivalent about the massive growth of urban centers and the emergence of major new urban political groups and often oppose policies that encourage these trends.

The export sector prefers laissez-faire policies for a number of reasons. The abandonment of free trade in favor of protective tariffs increases the costs of imported goods that this sector consumes, and subsidizes the emergence of manufacturing and industrial interests that ultimately emerge as major political adversaries of the exporters. With regard to the preferred system of property, the combined requirements of protecting their own wealth in a national setting of stark inequality and of having a sufficiently flexible system of control of land to allow them to expand production in response to changing world markets clearly point to the importance of a strong system of private property within the framework of a capitalist land market. With regard to taxation, the highly visible export enclaves are a natural target for government taxes, and the forms of government spending that are likely to be supported by these taxes tend to subsidize the emergence of urban, middle-class groups which also emerge eventually as political opponents of the export sector.

At the same time that the expansion of urban life represents a threat to the export sector, there is a clear ambivalence toward the urban economy and urban politics on the part of certain leading members of this sector which must be understood if one is to analyze settlement policy in the liberal period. This ambivalence comes out clearly in the complex variety of roles played by Pedro Beltrán, the leading spokesman of the liberal approach to squatter settlements. As the owner of a cotton hacienda and a major figure in the National Agrarian Society, Beltrán was one of the leading members of the export oligarchy[2] and the principal spokesman in Peru for the laissez-faire economic policies that were supported by this sector.[3] At the same time, he also had important commercial interests in urban areas. Apart from owning two newspapers—an important instrument of political power in the urban setting—Beltrán and other members of his family were involved in urban real estate and housing development, and he played a major role in the introduction of mutual savings and loan associations in Peru.[4] This particular combination of affiliations also comes out clearly in the case of Manuel Prado, an important political ally of the export sector who was president of Peru during the period when the liberal approach to settlements became official policy. Prado belonged to an elite family with major investments in real estate, commerce, and banking.[5] This particular alliance of economic sectors must be kept in mind, both in order to avoid an oversimplified conception of the conflict between rural and urban interests in Peru[6] and in order to interpret adequately the particular policies that Beltrán would support.

This chapter explores the relationship between these economic and political interests of individuals associated with these economic sectors and the liberal approach to settlement policy. It begins by examining the origins of this approach in the elite opposition to Odría during the first half of the 1950s. The development of this approach in the form of official housing proposals and official government policy during the period 1956 to 1960 is then analyzed.

The Opposition to Odría

When Odría came to power, he initially enjoyed the strong support of the export sector of the Peruvian oligarchy. This support was quickly repaid with decree laws that revised Peru's foreign exchange controls, thereby doubling the net profits of the export sector.[7] However, the close relations between Odría and this sector of the oligarchy were not to last. First of all, Odría abandoned his original commitment to form a short-term provisional government[8] and instead held a rigged election in 1950 through which he made himself constitutional president for a six-year term ending in 1956.[9] He might even have tried to stay on after 1956 had it not been for pressure from the oligarchy. Odría also abandoned the types of economic policies desired by the export oligarchy and gave considerable support to industrialization and to spending for public works.[10] He threatened the freedom of the elite-owned press, adopted what have been described as "gangster tactics" in forcing wealthy families to donate houses and other expensive gifts to government leaders,[11] and took advantage of certain provisions of the Internal Security Law to harass members of the oligarchy with whom he was quarreling.[12]

Another area of conflict between Odría and the elite involved Odría's support for squatter settlements that were involved in disputes with wealthy individuals who claimed the land occupied by the settlements. For instance, in 1955 a dispute arose between the residents of a settlement that had Odría's protection and Pedro Roselló, president of an association of owners of urban land (National Landowners Association). The government newspaper, *La Nación*, covered the dispute with a series of front-page stories accompanied by headlines printed in red ink. Every effort was made to present Roselló as an enemy of the people. Roselló was a close associate of the publisher and oligarch Pedro Beltrán, and counterstories appeared in Beltrán's newspaper *La Prensa* defending Roselló and the rights of private property. When Roselló decided to sell the disputed land for a symbolic price to the squatters who were occupying it, *La Prensa* and *Ultima Hora*, the afternoon tabloid owned by Beltrán, hailed Roselló as a friend of the people, whereas *La Nación* attacked him as a fraud for pretending to sell land that he did not own.[13] There were other instances of such disputes in which Odría sided with squatters, including one over part of the land on which the Twenty-seventh of October was located. Odría's position in these cases should not be interpreted as representing a radical policy that involved taking land from the rich and giving it to the poor, since the landowners who claimed these lands often had a rather dubious basis for their claims. However, Odría's tendency to side with the squatters clearly did represent an aggravation for urban landowners.

Odría's policies encouraging cityward migration were also inconsistent with the interests of the export oligarchy, which saw the growth of the urban sector as threatening to its interests. Odría's programs of urban public works and industrial development encouraged the development of the urban sector, and it was in part because of these programs that the export sector stopped supporting him.[14] Urban development represented less of an immediate threat to the elite of the highlands. This sector had already lost its dominant role in national politics and was concerned at this point primarily with maintaining control over local politics in the highlands. This control appeared to be enhanced by the urbanization that Odría was encouraging.

Beltrán's Housing Campaign

As relations between the export oligarchy and Odría worsened, Pedro Beltrán became an important leader of the opposition. Beltrán had played a major role in the anti-Apra campaign of the Bustamante period, as was noted above, and was a central member of the civilian group that supported Odría's coup. However, as Odría's policies began increasingly to conflict with elite interests, Beltrán and others became concerned with establishing a viable basis for opposing Odría. Beltrán chose to base this opposition on an issue that permitted vigorous attacks on the policies of Odría and at the same time appeared to offer an important means of gaining popular support—the issue of the shortage of low-cost housing. Beltrán launched a massive campaign dealing with problems of housing, carried out principally through his newspapers—*La Prensa* and *Ultima Hora.* He sought to underline the gravity of the housing shortage, the failure of the government to deal with the problem effectively, and the fact that many government housing policies were, in fact, counterproductive. He argued that housing built by the state could not contribute significantly to the solution of the housing problem and that the government should seek to encourage a larger role for private enterprise in building housing. He maintained that only the private sector had the capacity to produce enough new housing to meet the housing needs of the capital.[15]

In order to dramatize the gravity of the housing shortage in Lima and to publicize his proposed solutions, Beltrán became involved in sponsoring one of the largest settlement invasions ever to take place in Lima, that of the Ciudad de Dios, or City of God, settlement on Christmas Eve 1954. Evidence suggests that Beltrán was involved in sponsoring at least one other invasion in Cuzco as well. He thus chose to fight Odría on his own ground by supporting settlement formation.

Direct evidence about the sponsorship of the Lima invasion is hard to find, but most Peruvians who have had long experience with squatter settlements believe that Beltrán was involved. The circumstantial evidence is also striking. One of the principal leaders of the invasion was a man who had previously worked for Beltrán. In an interview with the author, a close associate of Beltrán, a man who had been involved in a land dispute with a settlement supported by Odría, praised the Ciudad de Dios invasion as one of high social purpose, at the same time referring to the "gangster tactics" employed in the invasions sponsored by Odría. *La Prensa* and *Ultima Hora* gave extensive coverage to the invasion, whereas the other papers paid little attention to it. *La Prensa* made frequent editorial reference to the invasion for years after it occurred, always citing it as evidence of the gravity of the housing shortage in Peru and of the need to follow the housing policies which *La Prensa* and Beltrán were proposing.[16] One of the editorials went so far as to refer enthusiastically to the invasion as "photogenic."[17] Since it would appear that Beltrán was well aware of the invasion before it occurred, it is ironical that another editorial referred to it as "surprising."[18] It was also described as surprising in the report of an important commission on problems of housing which was formed in the later 1950s and of which Beltrán was the president.[19]

The Ciudad de Dios invasion was used to publicize Beltrán's housing campaign in other ways as well. Beltrán played a central role in introducing mutual savings and loan associations in Peru in the 1950s. These were of interest to him both as a business venture and as part of his campaign to deal with the housing shortage. Curiously enough, the group in the Ciudad de Dios invasion, led by the man who was a former employee of Beltrán, called itself La Asociación Mutualista, or The Mutual Association, a name for a settlement association which the author has not encountered elsewhere.

Ciudad de Dios was also used to publicize Beltrán's concept of *la casa barata que crece* (the inexpensive house that grows). This was based on the idea of self-help development which had grown out of the experience of squatter settlements, and involved a small, nuclear house to which the occupant could add rooms when he had the resources and the inclination. *La Prensa* was raffling off these *casas baratas que crecen* during December 1954, just before the Ciudad de Dios invasion,[20] and it is interesting that a major pilot project that used this type of dwelling was constructed for the Ciudad de Dios residents after Prado, a close associate of Beltrán's, came to power in 1956.[21] *La Prensa* referred to 1955 as "the year of *la casa barata que crece*."[22] The concern with creating opportunities for self-help in housing development later became a major feature of Beltrán's housing proposals.

Finally, the Ciudad de Dios invasion was nicely coordinated to come just after the end of a major campaign concerning housing problems which ran in *La Prensa* from June through November of 1954. This involved twenty-two full-page weekly "bulletins" from the National Landowners Association, mentioned above. Using newspaper space donated by Beltrán, these bulletins stressed the gravity of the housing shortage and argued for changes in housing policy that would ease the shortage.

The Ciudad de Dios invasion thus represents a curious situation in which a leading member of the landed oligarchy, a class presumably deeply committed to the sanctity of private property, was involved in sponsoring a major settlement invasion. This same class had initially sponsored Odría's presidency, and its leaders must have been aware of Odría's activities in settlements before the coup of 1948. But it was one thing for the military protector of the oligarchy to get involved in settlements, and quite another for one of its leading members to be involved.

Though Odría and Beltrán both supported settlement formation, the contrast between the two men is striking. Odría was from a central Andean town, and his wife was a woman of humble origins.[23] Their identification with the poor and the migrants of the settlements must, to some degree, have been genuine. Beltrán, by contrast, has been described by Pike as "a fanatic of the right," a man who tended to "flaunt his . . . disdain for the lower classes," and who, after a period as prime minister in the late 1950s and early 1960s, emerged as "one of the most disliked figures that Peruvian politics had produced in many years."[24] Beltrán's involvement in settlements would thus seem to be well summarized by Gordon Tullock's ingenious phrase, "the charity of the uncharitable."[25]

How, then, can one explain Beltrán's involvement in this invasion and his concern more generally with settlements and housing problems? Two points may be noted. First, Odría had made it clear that settlements could be used as a source of political support, and Beltrán and his group were interested in seeking political support. Second, by giving so much attention to settlements and housing, Odría and Beltrán may have served to influence the way in which the problem of urban poverty has been treated as an issue in Peruvian politics. From the point of view of the political right, this was a desirable way for the problem of poverty to be treated, far more desirable than the more radical terms in which Apra had posed the problem, and one that lent itself to inexpensive solutions such as settlement formation.

It may be argued that Odría and Beltrán were attempting to define the issues and the nonissues of poverty in Lima in a way that was favorable to their interests.[26] Hirschman has argued that the "wily" reformer in Latin America may create opportunities to solve underlying social and economic problems by identifying them as the causes of other more immediate and pressing problems.[27] The present case, by contrast, involves a situation in which "wily" conservatives attempted to *divert* attention from underlying social and economic problems by making a major issue of housing. Improvements in housing helped to meet some of the more underlying problems of poverty, and yet could be achieved without drastic reform or large expenditures.

The question of the way in which the issues of Peruvian politics are defined became an explicit theme in political rhetoric in Peru in the later 1950s. Thus, while Beltrán liked to claim that housing was Peru's number one problem,[28] the left-leaning Social Progressive party countered at one point with a direct attack on Beltrán. The Social Progressives argued that "Peru's number one problem is not housing. It is poverty, which causes bad housing conditions, undernourishment, lack of education, poor health, and the lack of adequate clothing."[29] Whereas Beltrán saw in the issue of housing an inexpensive way of dealing with the problem of poverty, the Social Progressives were interested in the housing problem as an important symptom of poverty.[30]

Settlement Formation under Prado

Beginning in 1956, the liberal approach to squatter settlements began to play an important role in official policy. There was continuity with the Odría period in some aspects of policy, and certain features of settlement policy did not unambiguously represent a distinctively liberal approach. Nonetheless, the broad features of policy during the first four and a half years of the government of Manuel Prado clearly involved the application of the liberal approach to settlement policy.

Policy toward settlement formation during this period reflected to a greater degree the urban real estate, banking, and commercial interests that Prado represented. Hence, though extensive settlement formation continued under his government and though he occasionally supported it, Prado was more inclined to take the point of view of the landowner in reacting to squatter invasions and was more likely to use settlements in a way that favored elite commercial interests.

In comparison with the Odría period, the proportion of evictions, and of evictions and attempted evictions combined, was two and a half times as great during the Prado period (see Chapter III). If two settlements formed in this period and established legally under a law passed by the Congress in 1961 are excluded from the calculation, the proportions are even higher. There was also a higher proportion of settlements formed on disputed land—56 percent, as opposed to 17 percent under Bustamante and 30 percent under Odría. This may have been due to the fact that the government was quite willing to evict squatters from land that had a wealthy claimant, even if this contending claim had a rather dubious basis, a situation that obviously encouraged people to make such claims. In one infamous case, an evicted invasion group was required to make a large payment to a contending claimant before being permitted by the government to reoccupy the site. It later turned out that there was no basis for the claim, but by then the money had disappeared and was never returned.

The Prado government also encouraged the formation of new settlements as a means of making it easier to evict residents of inner-city slums. This type of authorization serves to aid real estate developers rather than to satisfy the needs of the poor, a use of settlements that one might expect under Prado, who was closely linked to real estate interests. Though this type of settlement formation has occurred under most governments, the involvement of the president was particularly close in Prado's case. This stands in clear contrast to Odría's tendency, noted in the last chapter, to take the side of settlement residents in eviction disputes.

Evidence about the Ciudad de Dios invasion suggests that Prado's commercial interests were already being served by settlement formation during the Odría period. It appears that the Ciudad de Dios invasion was used in part as a means of getting the residents out of certain inner-city slum areas owned by the Prado family. In one case during the Prado period, the government permitted a new settlement to form in order to make it easier to eradicate slum housing to make way for a new hospital. In two other cases, new settlements were formed in connection with the eradication of previously existing squatter settlements. One of these was a small peripheral settlement to the southeast of Lima which was located on

land claimed by a company owned by a relative of President Prado. After
a prolonged dispute, the entire community was invited to the Presidential
Palace to discuss the problem. They never got to see the president, but
when they returned home they found that their houses had been bull-
dozed to the ground. The government offered them land in another area
to form a new settlement.

A somewhat similar case involves an internal settlement, Uchumayo,
which gradually came to be surrounded by a middle-class neighborhood
and was subjected to pressure for eradication because it was considered
unattractive by the new neighbors. After a prolonged dispute, a fire
occurred in the settlement under circumstances that made it seem
extremely likely that it had been set as a way of getting rid of the
settlement. The fire damaged some of the houses, but did not actually
make it necessary for the families to abandon the site. The dispute over
the eradication continued, and finally the families were forced to leave
and were moved by the government, with direct approval from the
president, via the president's wife, to an area of unused land to the north
of Lima.

When the author interviewed the leaders of the settlement, a very
different story emerged initially. At first they said that they had been
driven from their homes by a terrible fire, and with great sentimentality
produced as evidence the charter of the neighborhood association of the
settlement which explained how the settlement had been formed. The
document stated that the settlement was formed "with the maternal
protection of the First Lady of Peru, Mrs. Clorinda Malaga de Prado." It
went on to say that the settlement had originally been named after her "in
demonstration of gratitude for her great efforts on our behalf in a
moment when we found ourselves in distress due to the voracious fire that
destroyed our humble homes, leaving us without shelter." After a brief
discussion of how terrible the fire had been, and how generous the
president's wife had been, there followed a more detailed discussion of
what had actually happened, and the real story emerged. At the end of the
conversation, they agreed that they had been evicted, rather than rescued,
by the wife of the president, but they couldn't quite come to terms with
the contradiction between this and what they had said at the beginning of
the conversation.

A while after this settlement was formed, the residents were invited by
a representative of Prado to meet with the president. They were picked up
in a truck at the appointed time, and were somewhat surprised when they
were taken to the airport to form part of a demonstration welcoming
Prado back from a trip abroad. They never got to speak to him. This

episode would seem to be an extraordinary instance of the way in which a myth of paternalistic generosity can mask manipulation of the poor. This paternalism and this use of settlements for political support was far less important under Prado than it had been under Odría, but it nonetheless did reappear occasionally.

At the same time that elite and middle-class interests influenced the formation of a number of settlements during this period, other kinds of pressure played a role as well. Because of the large number of settlements that were formed during the Odría period, many people had become aware of the opportunities offered by settlement formation. In response to these opportunities a new occupation was created, that of the *traficante*, the man who made a living working as an invasion leader and advisor to settlements on legal and other problems. Though these leaders made use of party and government linkages, they were usually quite ready to shift their political loyalties when the situation required. Two of the important *traficantes* of the Prado period had acquired their original experience in settlement formation in the invasions sponsored by Odría and Beltrán during the Odría period.

Apra also played a role during this period, though a somewhat ambiguous one. On the one hand, an Aprista was the head of a federation of settlement associations—the Frente Unico de Barriadas—which supported at least one invasion under Prado and one under the military government in 1963. This instance of support by a settlement federation has already been referred to in Chapter III, and is reported by Turner.[31] However, Apra was in an informal coalition with Prado and was often quite responsive to conservative interests. This is illustrated by a case in the late 1950s in which an invasion occurred near the highway to the east of Lima on a hill located next to a cemetery. To insure that the squatters would be evicted, the Apra union in a nearby factory made a false claim to the land. After a prolonged dispute, the squatters were moved to another area.

Settlement Policy and Housing Policy

The Prado period was a time of extensive concern with settlement policy and with housing policy more generally. As in the Odría period, Pedro Beltrán played a major role in the debate. Prado's Supreme Decree Number One of 10 August 1956 created a Commission on Agrarian Reform and Housing, with Beltrán as president.[32] Later, as prime minister under Prado starting in 1959, Beltrán had an opportunity to try out a number of his proposals for housing and settlement policy, primarily through a new housing office founded in 1960, the Instituto Nacional de la Vivienda.[33]

Interest in problems of settlements and housing was by no means restricted to Beltrán, however. Problems of housing were widely discussed in the press, and not solely in Beltrán's papers, *La Prensa* and *Ultima Hora*. In addition to two major studies of housing published by the Beltrán Commission, two important studies of settlements were also carried out in this period.[34] The issue of settlements was extensively discussed in the Congress, and Apra took a particularly active role in the debate, sponsoring a conference on problems of settlements and introducing a new name for settlements, "town in formation" (*pueblo en formación*), to replace the somewhat derogatory terms that had previously been applied to settlements.[35] Housing and settlements clearly had become major issues in Peruvian politics.

In the context of this debate, Pedro Beltrán played a major role in changing settlement policy and housing policy in Peru. He argued that traditional public housing could, at best, make only a marginal contribution to solving the housing problem and that rent control and excessively high zoning standards had been counterproductive. The two most important components of the alternative program that Beltrán proposed involved encouraging the role of the private sector in increasing the supply of housing and increasing opportunities for housing development based on self-help.[36]

In Beltrán's program, the role of the private sector would be stimulated through the elimination of rent control; tax incentives for the construction of low-income housing; changes in the tax on real estate transactions to make it more equitable for transactions involving small properties; easing the requirements for qualifying for a mortgage and introducing mortgage insurance; encouraging mutual savings and loan associations; and special incentives for private investment which would help to lower the cost of land.[37] Self-help would be encouraged both through building types of housing developments that lent themselves to self-help and cooperation among neighbors and through providing technical assistance to guide self-help efforts. Beltrán particularly emphasized the value of self-help in squatter settlements and urged that once community improvements had been carried out on the basis of self-help, land titles should be granted.[38] Squatter settlements would thus be incorporated within the conventional system of private property. Beltrán also proposed a program of mutual aid through which groups of up to fifteen to twenty families could work together to build all of their houses at once, with technical assistance from the state to guide their efforts.[39] Another important part of Beltrán's program was the *casa barata que crece*, the inexpensive house that grows. This concept combined the two aspects of Beltrán's approach to housing, since it was a housing unit that could be produced by the private sector and that also lent itself to self-help.

Beltrán's ideas about housing policy were brought together in a proposal for comprehensive new housing legislation which was contained in the *Report on Housing in Peru* of the Beltrán Commission, published in 1958. The law would create a new national housing administration which would coordinate the activities of existing agencies that dealt with housing and form and supervise other agencies that would develop Beltrán's programs for encouraging the role of the private sector in housing. The proposed law also stipulated that the local municipal governments should be given a major role in housing development.[40]

Beltrán's housing campaign constantly emphasized the idea that as many Peruvian families as possible should become homeowners, that each should have its own house, its *casa propia*. This goal was mentioned at the beginning of the Supreme Decree that created the Beltrán Commission,[41] and periodic references were made in Beltrán's newspapers and in promotional literature for the mutual funds to the ideal of having a *casa propia*, the dream of having a *casa propia*, and the goal of a *casa propia* for all Peruvians. When Beltrán became prime minister, he introduced another slogan, *Techo y Tierra*, or Roof and Land, as the name for his program of urban and rural development.[42]

In making a major political issue of providing a *casa propia* for all Peruvians, Beltrán was responding to a basic and strongly felt desire of the lower class. The remarkable importance of homeownership to lower-income groups in Lima is strikingly reflected in a survey of industrial workers in greater Lima conducted in 1962–63.[43] In response to a question regarding their most important personal goal, 54 percent of the sample indicated that it was homeownership, a *casa propia*. By contrast, only 9.9 percent said permanent work, 9.7 percent said a good economic situation, and 8.6 percent said good health. All three of these alternative responses represented goals that one might expect to be very important, and yet the response of homeownership is twice as frequent as all of the other three combined.

Beltrán's Strategy of Incorporation

Peruvians who are knowledgeable about the history of housing policy in Peru agree that in seeking to help the urban poor to satisfy this desire for homeownership, Beltrán was pursuing a well-defined set of broader goals. It is felt that Beltrán believed that if the poor have desirable housing which they own and which they can improve themselves, this will tie them into the system, increase their respect for private property, and make them less susceptible to radical appeals and less dependent on the state. Some of these ideas are expressed in the Preliminary Report of the Beltrán Commission, which argued that

> "property . . . serves the purpose of securing for the man and his family economic autonomy in the face of renewed and growing needs, and *independence with respect to the state*. Hence, any housing . . . program has a substantive personal and social significance which should be taken into account. *The development of responsible individuals . . . [is] an essential complement to any program for the increase of ownership."*[44] [Emphasis added in this and the following three quotations.]

Beltrán's approach to incorporating the poor was thus precisely the opposite from Odría's. Through charity and paternalism, Odría increased the dependence of the poor on the state. The failure to grant land titles in settlements heightened this dependence. Beltrán, on the other hand, sought to reduce this dependence through the creation of self-sufficient communities of small property owners. Odría's links with the traditional agriculture of the highlands and the important parallel between the semifeudal, precapitalist economic relationships that existed in the traditional latifundia and Odría's lack of commitment to granting land titles in settlements were noted in Chapter IV. Beltrán, by contrast, represented Peru's leading capitalist sector and was the most prominent spokesman for capitalism in Peru. Since private property is the basis for capitalism, Beltrán's commitment to private property in settlements is hardly surprising.

Apart from the question of homeownership, the final *Report on Housing in Peru* of the Beltrán Commission discussed with surprising clarity the political consequences of a desirable home environment and of self-help housing development. These arguments regarding the consequences of living in a settlement are quite similar to those presented above in Chapter II. The Beltrán report emphasized the advantages of

> a healthy and normal family life within a propitious environment, consisting primarily of the home, the neighborhood, and the local community. . . . Family life under these circumstances not only *strengthens the moral fiber of the members* . . . but is *conducive to emotional stability* . . . *and minimizes social conflict.* . . . *All these factors contribute to the country's security and stability.* . . .[45]

A related idea is expressed in another section of the report concerned with the role of the state in constructing housing. Though the report emphasized that the state could not by itself solve the housing problem, it suggested that some state-supported housing would be necessary. In discussing the advantages of the "decent and healthful" houses that the state would offer, the report emphasizes that

> state housing not only should seek to place a decent dwelling at the disposal of families who cannot afford one but to provide a social education as well. . . . [T]he educational effort should *inculcate in the people the conviction that only through their own efforts to raise their economic level will they be able to cease to depend on state support in the form of these dwellings, and to achieve a better life.*[46]

In a discussion of the merits of self-help and community development projects in settlements, the report argues that

> one of the best ways to form an active and responsible citizenry is to organize community work methods in such a way as to promote individual initiative and insure the participation of all members of the community in the analysis and solution of their own problems. *Through this process of self-education, conscientious and progressive communities are formed which seek to attend to their own affairs, making use of whatever resources they have at hand and not waiting for everything to be provided by the government or some other authority.*[47]

The message is clear. Better housing and self-help produce emotional stability; reduce social conflct; contribute to the country's security and stability; teach the poor to attend to their own affairs and make use of the resources that are at hand; and convince them that only through their own efforts, and not through aid from the state or through radical politics, can they achieve a better life.

The type of family and community life that Beltrán was trying to promote is reminiscent of Karl Marx's famous characterization of the nineteenth-century small-holding peasants in France as resembling "potatoes in a sack" in their inability to join together as an economic and political class. Marx argued that because "there is merely a local interconnection among these small-holding peasants, and the identity of their interests begets no community, no national bond and no political organization among them, they do not form a class. They are consequently incapable of enforcing their class interest. . . ."[48] The quotations from the Beltrán Commission Report suggest that Beltrán was similarly interested in inhibiting the development and political expression of class interests among the poor of Lima.

This strategy of incorporation was, of course, not the only goal that Beltrán sought to promote through his housing and settlement policies. The emphasis in his policies on encouraging the role of the private sector

in housing development clearly served commercial and real estate interests with which he had not only a close relation but also a direct involvement through his role in mutual funds and real estate developments.
The Prado family was also extensively involved in urban real estate. In
addition, Roselló, who was closely associated with Beltrán's housing
campaign, was the owner of a company that sold materials for home
construction. Thus the housing campaign, like many of the cases of settlement formation under Prado, served the business interests of those
who supported it.

Settlement Policy, Urbanization, and Agrarian Reform

It has already been argued that there are important links and trade-offs
between settlement policy and rural development policy. These links are
particularly interesting in the liberal period. It was suggested above that
one of the important reasons for the split between Odría and the export
oligarchy was the tendency of some of Odría's policies to encourage
urbanization and thereby favor the implicit interests of the traditional
oligarchy over the export oligarchy by easing the pressure for change in
the rural areas of traditional agriculture. Though the export oligarchy
had previously been willing to protect the interests of the traditional
oligarchy of the highlands, by the end of the Odría period the traditional
order of the highlands was so nearly on the verge of collapse that the
coastal elite shifted its position.[49] In the face of this crisis, the coastal elite
proposed agrarian reform in areas of traditional agriculture.[50] The
creation of the Commission on Agrarian Reform and Housing in 1956
clearly marked the end of the period in which agrarian reform had been a
forbidden issue in Peruvian politics.[51] The commission became the
channel through which the proposals of the export elite for rural change
were developed.

In rural areas, as in urban areas, a major goal of the commission was to
encourage the ownership of property among the middle and lower classes.
The opening sentence of the decree that created the commission declared
that "small and intermediate property should constitute the foundation of
the economic and social structure of the country."[52] The Preliminary
Report of the commission of August 1956 proposed that in order to
achieve this aim, the state should "purchase and subdivide unproductive
large land holdings . . . [and] haciendas in regions of heavy population
density and rural property concentration."[53] The references to unproductive holdings and heavy population density were intended to limit the
reform to the areas of traditional agriculture of the highlands, excluding

from the proposed reform the export-oriented haciendas of the coast and certain large, modern haciendas in the highlands.

The program proposed by the commission was intended to achieve a number of goals. It was suggested above that one of the reasons for Beltrán's interest in promoting urban homeownership was his belief that it makes people more conservative and less dependent on the state. The same principle also applied to rural landownership. In order to deal with the shortage of arable land, the Preliminary Report argued that it was necessary to extend irrigation to areas of desert land, subdivide and sell unused state property, and open up new areas of agriculture in the eastern jungle region of Peru through colonization projects.[54] Thus, in addition to introducing a system of rural property holding that would have a conservatizing effect on the peasantry, Beltrán also sought to solve the agrarian crisis by making more land available for cultivation in all areas of Peru. During his term as prime minister, Beltrán actively supported both agrarian reform and programs for the colonization of the jungle.[55]

Taken together, the proposals of the Beltrán Commission represent a highly sophisticated response to the threat to the position of the coastal oligarchy. By abandoning the oligarchy of the highlands and proposing agrarian reform, it would presumably be possible to ease the migratory pressure on Lima and thereby inhibit the growth of the social sectors which ultimately posed the greatest threat to the export oligarchy. Landownership would ensure the continued conservative orientation of the peasants who stayed in the areas of traditional agriculture, and those who chose migration would be attracted to other rural areas, instead of the cities, by irrigation and colonization programs.

In view of the fact that Beltrán had sponsored a major settlement invasion, it is clear that he did not go as far as Belaúnde and Velasco would later go in opposing settlements and urban growth—though he did occasionally pronounce against the alarming growth of settlements in the pages of *La Prensa*. Rather, he saw, on the one hand, opportunities for diverting migration from Lima, and, on the other hand, the opportunity to instill in the urban lower class the virtues of self-reliance which would reduce their dependence on the state and decrease the likelihood of future demands for massive state programs.

Conclusion

The approach to settlement policy of the liberal period was quite distinct from that which had characterized the Odría period. In place of dependence and informality, the purpose in this period was to make the settlement residents *in*dependent of the state and to create a highly structured world of property ownership and self-help that would teach the poor to take care of themselves and reduce their availability for mobilization into disruptive political movements. Because settlement policy in the liberal period included this alternative strategy for limiting pluralism, it can be viewed as one component of a second approach to authoritarian rule which was quite distinct from that which appeared under Odría.

VI

Sweeping Policy Commitments:
The Period of Party Politics

The late 1950s and particularly the 1960s were a period in which mass-based political parties played an increasingly important role in making settlement policy. The 1956 presidential election had been, in considerable measure, a contest between two members of the elite. Party politics had played some role, but Apra had not been allowed to resume normal party activity until shortly before the election, and the outcome hinged in large part on which of the elite candidates could offer the best deal in which Apra would once again be legalized in exchange for votes in the election.[1] Once the election had taken place, however, party politics became a much more central feature of the Peruvian political scene. Apra now appeared to be more ready to play the role of a conventional political party within the Peruvian party system; the Popular Action party had a wide following; and other parties—including the Christian Democrats, the Social Progressives, and the Communist Party—came to play an active role in Peruvian politics in the later 1950s and early 1960s. It appeared that there would be relatively free party competition in the 1962 presidential elections, and much of the legislative and party politics of this period was oriented toward building support for these elections.

One of the most important implications for settlement policy of this new period of party politics can be summarized quite simply: "Teach the poor to take care of themselves" does not make a very good electoral slogan in a country in which the mass of the population—and of the voting population—is poor. The spectacular failure of Beltrán's attempt to launch a presidential campaign with an eye to the 1962 elections clearly attested to the limited electoral appeal of this approach.[2] The demands of party competition inclined the political parties instead toward sweeping

policy commitments that were quite distinct from the approach of
Beltrán. In terms of the generic type of policy orientation that emerged, it
involved a shift from what was described above as a "conventional"
approach to a "democratic reform" approach, based on a larger and more
active role of the state.[3]

The period of party politics, like the liberal period, did not bring a total
discontinuity in the approach to settlement policy. The debate in settlement policy of the mid-1950s which had been led by Beltrán and in which
Apra had played a part defined the broad framework within which
subsequent policy making developed. There were clear differences, however, in the overall orientation of policy.

Law 13517, passed by the Congress in February of 1961, is the most
important example of the new approach to settlement policy.[4] This law
evolved out of the work in settlements of the National Housing Corporation, a state housing agency founded in the 1940s, and was drafted by
officials of this agency and by leading legislators, particularly Senator
Arca Parró, who, though not an Apra member, was associated with Apra.
The law embodied many of Beltrán's ideas about remodeling and
legalizing settlements and forming new housing projects based on the
principle of self-help.[5] However, it did not include Beltrán's program for
expanding the role of the private sector in housing development, and it
made far more sweeping commitments to government programs in
settlements than were favored by Beltrán.

Apart from these differences in the basic approach to the problem of
housing and settlements, the question of who would get credit for the new
legislation was also an important issue in this preelection period. Since
Beltrán had presidential ambitions, the political parties represented in the
Congress did not want him to get credit for the new housing legislation
and sought to pass a law that would not be identified with him.[6] As it
became clear that Beltrán's proposals would not be accepted by the
Congress, Prado created by Supreme Decree the National Housing
Institute, which Beltrán used as a vehicle for applying his housing
proposals.[7] Beltrán thus had his own housing agency which was clearly
identified with his housing proposals and through which he began actively
to carry out these proposals. It is ironical that this period of the most
active application of his ideas came after his approach had lost out in the
legislative struggle in the Congress.

Law 13517

Law 13517 introduced another new name for settlements, "marginal
neighborhoods" (*barrios marginales*), seeking, as Apra had done earlier,

to use a new name to signal a fresh approach to policy. The two basic purposes of the law were to offer an alternative to the illegal formation of settlements and to provide for the remodeling and legalization of existing settlements. The formation of new settlements through invasions was explicitly prohibited by Article 2 of the law, and settlements formed through invasion after 20 September 1960 were excluded from receiving benefits under the law. As an alternative to invasions, Article 3 gave the National Housing Corporation (CNV) the authority to form new settlements called *urbanizaciones populares* (lower-class housing projects) in which the agency would lay out street grids, install services, and build a rudimentary house on each lot. It emphasized that self-help and community projects were to play an important role in the development of these *urbanizaciones*. The residents, who would apply for lots through the CNV, were to move in and proceed to expand their houses as they would in any squatter settlement. However, they would have the advantage of doing it on level ground (some of the early settlements were on hillsides) on which streets, water, sewage, and electricity had been installed *prior* to their arrival, and with the benefit of careful control of lot size and of the number of lots in each settlement. The residents would pay on a long-term basis for the services and the land, receiving full title only when their payments were completed.

Article 10.03 of the enabling legislation (*Reglamento*) for Law 13517, which was approved in July of 1961,[8] considerably broadened the potential scope of the *urbanización popular* program by extending the authority to establish these communities to local governments and to any nonprofit group that would form them in conformity with 13517—that is to say, not by invasions. This provision would later prove to be important in the context of the democratization of local government under Belaúnde. Article 10.04 of the *Reglamento* authorized the CNV to form an *urbanización popular* any time there was a proven demand for it. These two articles thus provided the legal basis for extensive government involvement in settlement formation.

In addition to providing for the formation of new settlements, the law set up a procedure for remodeling and granting land titles in the settlements that had already been formed. Prior to legalization, city services had to be installed and, in settlements that lacked an orderly street grid and a uniform lot size, remodeling had to be carried out. The residents were to pay for the cost of services and remodeling over a number of years and, as indicated above, would not receive full title until payments were completed. If the settlement was on public land, they would pay a symbolic price for the land. If the land was private and had to be expropriated, each family would pay its share of the cost of expropriation.

Since this law and its *Reglamento* legalized the formation of settlements, it would appear to be quite a radical measure. Article 10.01 of the
Reglamento also specified an income level below which families had to
fall to be eligible to move to the *urbanizaciones populares*. In this sense,
the law specified a class of people, in economic terms, who were eligible to
receive benefits under it. The law was not really economically redistribu-
tive, however, since in both the remodeled settlements and the *urbanizaciones populares* the residents were to pay the full cost of the installation
of services. However, certain articles clearly favored the residents. It was
significant that in settlements that had been formed on public land, the
residents would pay only a symbolic price for the land. In cases in which
settlements had been formed on private land, the land was to be
expropriated and payment made to the owner for an amount equivalent
to its estimated value at the time of formation, rather than at the time of
the expropriation. Because of rising land values, this involved a much
smaller sum of money in most cases. Since most of the communities
conventionally defined as settlements were not on private land, this would
not appear to be a significant feature of the law. However, Article 27
stated that communities that physically resembled squatter settlements
and in which the residents had built their houses on rented land would
be included in the definition of settlements and would be eligible for
expropriation and benefits under the law. This included a large number of
slum areas near the center of Lima which were originally settled through
the renting of lots to families who then built shacks on them, and in some
cases in turn subdivided and sublet the lots. The inclusion of these
communities was certainly the most radical part of the law, and it meant
that the favorable (from the squatters' point of view) terms of expropriation provided by the law had much wider application than they would
otherwise have had.

Apart from these specific provisions, the overall significance of Law
13517 was that it represented a formal commitment to pursue policies that
had previously been applied on a very informal and discretionary basis.
The government had previously supported settlement formation and had
given various kinds of aid to settlements. It was now committed to form
new settlements any time there was a proven demand and to remodel and
legalize all previously existing settlements.

This policy thus differed from the policy of the liberal period in that
the government was committed to making a major contribution to settlement development. It differed from the Odría period in that, at least
at the level of statute, this commitment was far less personalistic, since a
clearly defined category of people was identified who were declared
eligible to receive assistance.

During the last year of the Prado government after the passage of 13517, the CNV received substantial financial and political support and was able to start three large *urbanizaciones populares* which by the late 1960s had a population of roughly twenty thousand. However, problems quickly emerged in the application of the law. Following the passage of the law, the residents of a number of slum communities in Lima stopped paying rent in the hope that their communities would be recognized as settlements under Article 27. In many cases they did not qualify, and to resolve these disputes the government offered these families land in the *urbanizaciones populares*, so that a substantial proportion of the new lots were quickly taken up simply for the purpose of settling these disputes.

Evidence from interviews suggested that these slum communities had been encouraged to stop paying rent by a coalition of leaders from different settlements led by the same member of Apra referred to earlier who had been involved in supporting invasions. This group had also arranged demonstrations to demand passage of Law 13517 and its *Reglamento*, though informed sources suggest that these demonstrations had little influence on the Congress. However, it is clear that these rent strikes did create considerable difficulties for the CNV, and in this sense this group had a significant impact on the application of the law.

The Military Government of 1962–63

The period of military rule from 1962 to 1963 saw a continuation of political support for the provisions of Law 13517, as well as an interesting episode in which one of the leaders of this government briefly, and unsuccessfully, attempted to follow Odría's example in creating a base of personal support in the squatter settlements. Prado's second term ended in 1962, and the presidential elections of June of that year failed to produce a clear victory for either Apra or the other two principal candidates, Odría and Belaúnde.[9] Under the Peruvian constitution, the choice of president therefore went to the Congress, and it appeared likely that a bizarre coalition would emerge in which Apra would throw its support to Odría, giving him enough votes to be elected president.[10] The military reacted to this prospect with a coup on 18 July.[11] Claiming electoral fraud, they were in fact anxious to prevent the opportunistic coalition of former enemies. This may be explained in part by the armed forces' traditional enmity for Apra, but also in terms of a profound change that was occurring in the orientation of the Peruvian military. They no longer viewed themselves as protectors of the status quo, but rather believed that Peru urgently needed reform.[12] They therefore preferred the only viable reformist candidate, Belaúnde, and took power with the intention of holding elections in the near future in the hope of insuring Belaúnde's victory. This military government was thus distinct from the government of Odría. It was anti-Apra, but it did not repress Apra—though at one point it did suspend constitutional guarantees and arrest a large number of leftists.[13] Also, it was interested in reform and introduced several important reform measures during its year in power.[14]

The military government was strongly committed to forceful application of Law 13517, and supported the role of the private sector in housing development through the formation of a national housing bank, the Banco de la Vivienda, which replaced a temporary agency that had been part of the National Housing Institute.[15] They saw the overlapping responsibilities of the National Housing Corporation and the National Housing Institute as wasteful and combined them in a single agency, the Junta Nacional de la Vivienda (JNV). The government's commitment to keeping the growth of settlements within the legal channels provided by Law 13517 was reflected in several violent evictions that took place during this period. As was shown in Chapter III, 43 percent of the cases in the smaller sample in this period involved evictions and 57 percent involved evictions or serious attempts to evict. If one excludes from the calculation the *urbanización popular* formed under Law 13517 which was established during this period, the percentages rise to 50 and 66.

Unlike Odría, this government was not interested in seeking popular support in the settlements. There seem to be two reasons for this. First, since its purpose was not to rule over an extended period, but rather to act as a caretaker government until new elections were held, it did not have to concern itself with popular support in the way Odría did. Secondly, it considered itself to be a government of the military as an institution, and not of a single military leader.[16] When it appeared that Pérez-Godoy, the first president under the military government, was moving toward personalistic rule, he was removed from power in order to preserve the institutional character of the government.[17] This episode takes on particular interest in the present context because of Pérez-Godoy's relationship with squatter settlements. According to information collected in the survey of settlement formation, a close associate of Pérez-Godoy's was recruiting people to carry out squatter invasions in late 1962. This was obviously part of his attempted move toward personal rule, and was reminiscent of the tactics of Odría. Pérez-Godoy's interest in settlements is hardly surprising in light of the fact that he had been involved in the Odría government. It is noteworthy that during the Odría period, the headquarters of the settlement association of the Twenty-seventh of October displayed, along with pictures of Odría and his wife and Perón and his wife, a picture of Pérez-Godoy.[18]

The Belaúnde Government

The events of the Belaúnde period, from 1963 to 1968, bring into clear focus the risks of policy failure that accompany the kinds of policy commitments that emerged in the period of party politics. Fernando Belaúnde Terry came to power after the new elections that were held in June of 1963. Belaúnde had strong support from the Lima middle and upper-middle class, and also made a major electoral appeal to rural areas, carrying his campaign to remote Andean communities.[19] Belaúnde's development program accordingly focused on rural Peru. He believed that Peru suffered from serious overcentralization and he desired to divert resources away from Lima.[20] Through the building of a major highway along the edge of the Amazonian jungle to the east of the Andes and other measures of rural development, Belaúnde hoped to end the traditional pattern of migration from the highlands to the coast by encouraging migrants to move instead to the underpopulated regions to the east of the Andes.[21] A proposed agrarian reform would likewise ease the migratory pressure on Lima by giving many peasants access to land and thereby increasing the incentive to remain in the highlands.

Both Belaúnde's base of popular support and his development program made it improbable that he would have much interest in squatter settlements. The main thrust of his attempt to get popular support from the lower classes was directed at rural, not urban, areas. He likewise believed that the expenditure of resources to improve squatter settlements in urban areas would only attract more migrants to the cities, thus counteracting the positive effect of his other programs.[22]

Another reason for his lack of interest in settlements may have been Belaúnde's background as an architect and city planner. Though he brought progressive ideas to many areas of policy, he had been identified with the traditional approach to housing shortages that emphasized conventional public housing projects, having himself planned an important middle- to low-income project that was constructed in the late 1940s. During Belaúnde's term as president, the most important government investments in housing had little relation to the housing needs of the poor. Instead, the emphasis was on handsomely designed projects for middle- and upper-middle-class families. This choice may in part be attributed to the nature of Belaúnde's base of political support in urban areas, which came much more from the middle and upper-middle classes than from the poor. It is noteworthy that some of the residents of the slums that were eradicated to make way for the most visible of these projects, San Filipe, were relocated in settlements.

Because of lack of support from Belaúnde, and because of opposition from the majority coalition in Congress formed by Apra and the supporters of Odría, the program to apply Law 13517 quickly lost momentum.[23] The disputes that arose in connection with Article 27, which was responsible for the rent strikes in a number of inner-city slums, likewise hurt the program. By 1967, Congress had cut the appropriation for the JNV to 11 percent of its 1963 level.[24] In the face of this loss of resources, the JNV chose to limit its program to certain peripheral settlements that required less remodeling, hence drastically limiting the scope of its efforts. Its program was also inhibited by the fact that legalization had to await installation of services. Without funds to pay the initial costs of the services and remodeling, legalization could not proceed.

Plans to acquire extensive areas of land for the formation of additional *urbanizaciones populares* were dropped because of lack of support from Belaúnde and congressional opposition. Two additional *urbanizaciones populares* were formed to the north of Lima, but because of lack of funds no services were installed, and these communities in every way resembled conventional invasion sites in an early stage of development. Another area to the south of Lima, which the JNV had intended to reserve as a zone for light industry that would provide employment for settlement residents, ended up being filled with new settlements, in part through invasions, and in part by groups that the JNV moved there as a way of settling eradication disputes in inner-city slums. No services were provided in these areas either.

Because of the glaring contrast between the high hopes stimulated by Law 13517 and the JNV's failure to develop the *urbanización popular* plan as intended and to remodel and legalize the existing settlements, the agency was widely hated in the settlements by the end of the 1960s. Some have suggested that an aloof, technocratic attitude adopted by many JNV officials toward settlement residents reinforced the residents' opinion of the agency.

One important innovation of the JNV in the late 1960s should, however, be noted. In an attempt to deal with the problem of the lack of funds, the JNV set up an *urbanización popular*, Chacra Cerro, in which a private bank took direct responsibility for arranging periodic payments by the residents for their lots. This arrangement was reminiscent of the more active coordination with the private sector which Beltrán had promoted, and anticipated the government's encouragement of the role of banks in settlements after 1968.

Though Belaúnde's concern with decentralization meant less attention to settlements in national policy, it had the opposite effect at the level of local government in Lima. One of the most important aspects of Belaúnde's program of decentralization was to make local government in

Peru elective, rather than appointive.[25] This reform, along with the formation of several new political districts for squatter settlement areas, led to a far greater vitality of local politics in the settlements. During this period when settlement policy was in considerable measure shaped by the needs of political parties, party politics at the local, as well as the national, level came to play an important role in influencing settlement policy.

The role of local party politics became particularly evident with the approach of the elections of 1969, as contending parties vied to see which could offer the most attractive program to the settlements. In light of the JNV's difficulties in carrying out the program to legalize settlements, it is hardly surprising that legalization became a major issue. In 1967, Enrique León Velarde, mayor of the district which was formerly the Twenty-seventh of October and had been renamed San Martín de Porras at the beginning of the Prado period, successfully pushed for the passage of a law that eliminated remodeling as a requirement for granting titles in his district.[26] In mid-1968, in the face of a threatened march by settlement residents to the central plaza of Lima, to be led by León Velarde, further decrees were promulgated which extended this innovation to all settlements.[27] On the basis of these new laws, there was a brief upsurge in the granting of land titles at the end of the Belaúnde period, since it could proceed without the expensive remodeling that had previously been required.

This was a significant innovation in two senses. First, it represents one of the important occasions on which pressure mobilized from below was the immediate cause of a change in settlement policy. Secondly, it involves a basic issue of settlement policy in Peru and other countries: the extent to which traditional planners' standards are relaxed in recognition of the contribution of settlements to urban development.[28] Law 13517 took an important step toward accepting settlements as a normal aspect of urban housing development. However, the legalization procedure established by the law was to be applied only after the installation of services and remodeling—hence after the settlements had been brought more nearly into conformity with conventional planners' standards. The Beltrán Commission Report had recommended a similar prerequisite for legalization.[29] The laws of 1967 and 1968 departed completely from this approach, permitting the legalization of settlements without remodeling and services and taking Peru unusually far in the direction of abandoning traditional planners' standards in the interest of legalization.

The increase in party activity in settlements also resulted in the emergence of new kinds of partisan games in connection with squatter invasions. Four settlements formed during this period were authorized by municipal governments, which claimed authority to form settlements under the *Reglamento* of Law 13517.[30] Because Apra controlled certain municipal governments, this gave Apra a legal channel for supporting settlement formation. Another invasion was used as part of the partisan struggle between Apra and Enrique León Velarde. In 1968, Apra arranged an invasion of some land that was thought to belong to León Velarde, the purpose being to force him to call the police to evict the invaders, thereby discrediting him as a friend of the poor.

Because of the active sponsorship of settlements by the municipal governments and the JNV, government-sponsored settlements absorbed most of the pressure for the formation of new settlements during the Belaúnde period, and there were few invasions (see Chapter III). The fact that the district governments provided a channel through which Apra could sponsor settlements also contributed to the lack of invasions. The proportion of evictions and attempted evictions was correspondingly low during this period, only 22 percent.

One spectacular case in which the government did make an energetic attempt to evict occurred in October of 1963, shortly after Belaúnde had come to office. Though there were various reasons for the strong police reaction, a major factor was the widespread peasant land seizures in rural areas in the highlands, which were occurring in anticipation of the agrarian reform that Belaúnde had promised. These land seizures received massive coverage in the Lima press, particularly in *La Prensa*, and were a great embarrassment to the government. When a major squatter invasion occurred in Lima in the same week in which the rural land seizures were receiving such wide attention, the government was under particularly strong pressure to act firmly against the squatters. As will be shown in the next chapter, rural instability would again influence the government's response to urban invasions under the Velasco government.

A Strategy of Incorporation?

In the first two policy periods considered in this analysis—the periods of paternalism and liberalism—there appears to have been a relatively well defined strategy of incorporation reflected in settlement policy—a relatively well defined strategy for linking the urban poor to the national political system. A central purpose of the strategy in each period has been the limitation of pluralism and, correspondingly, these strategies have been interpreted as reflecting one aspect of authoritarian rule in Peru.

During the period of party politics, it would seem that the strategy of incorporation involved the attempt to win electoral support in exchange for benefits allocated through public policy. Political control was not a central element in the same way it was in the other periods. Party politics in the Peruvian context may, in some ways, have the latent function of limiting pluralism. The kind of distributive politics that political parties promote in Peru may be a central part of the pattern of "segmentary incorporation" through which the most advanced elements of new social sectors are brought into the system in a way that makes them more interested in increasing their own immediate material benefits than in broadening their mass base.[31] Similarly, to the extent that the principal centrist and reformist parties take votes and other kinds of support away from parties of the extreme left, it may serve to limit pluralism in a certain sense. However, this is hardly comparable to the carefully articulated strategy of Beltrán or the manifest intent of Odría's coup to end the style of party competition that Apra had been promoting between 1945 and 1948. Thus, settlement policy during the period of party politics did reflect a clear strategy of incorporation, but, in contrast to the other periods, the limitation of pluralism, and hence authoritarian rule, was not a central component of that strategy.

This is not to say that Peru was not, in certain important ways, an authoritarian political system during this period. However, the strategy of incorporation reflected in settlement policy was primarily focused on gaining electoral support—rather than political control. In this sense, this period is quite distinct from the other three periods analyzed in this study.

Conclusion

The period of party politics was hardly homogeneous in terms of the kind of settlement policy it produced. It combined the sweeping commitments of Law 13517 with the neglect of settlements under Belaúnde. It also combined the prohibition of new invasions in this law and the partial enforcement of this provision by two different governments with a new pattern of invasions that was directly linked to party competition. Yet policy clearly diverged from the liberal period in terms of the sweeping nature of the policy commitments that flowed from Law 13517. It diverged from the Odría period in that the government role in the settlements was formalized in law, instead of being informal and paternalistic. In addition, it diverged from both of the previous periods of settlement policy in that it did not include an explicit strategy for limiting political pluralism in Peru. This phase of settlement policy thus does not correspond to a distinct phase of authoritarian rule. This should hardly be surprising, given the fact that this was a period in which intense competition among political parties was a central feature of the political scene.

With regard to policy performance, a dominant theme of this period is the failure to carry out sweeping policy commitments, because of a fundamental difference between the approach to settlements of Belaúnde and of the authors of the law, and also because of the fragmenting effect of party competition itself. This produced a pattern of policy failure and of disillusionment with settlement policy which involved precisely the kinds of negative consequences of sweeping policy commitments against which Beltrán had warned. A central concern of settlement policy since 1968 has been to deal with these issues of policy failure and disillusionment.

VII

Self-Help and Comprehensive Political Control: Settlement Policy under Velasco

In the 1960s Peru experienced a failure to institute reform and a series of crises which, taken together, had an even greater impact on Peruvian political life than the crises of the 1940s.[1] These new crises resulted in considerable measure from a stalemate among the principal political groups considered in this study. In the context of the lingering power of the export oligarchy and the tenacious partisan opposition of Apra, few of the reforms proposed by the Belaúnde government were realized—reforms that were strongly supported by the Peruvian military. The peasant land seizures of the early 1960s, the rural guerrilla movement of the mid-1960s, and the specter of an urban guerrilla movement which was raised by the experience of other Latin American countries also contributed to the crisis. Still another factor was the crisis of legitimacy of the Peruvian political system produced in the late Belaúnde period by major smuggling scandals and by the scandal surrounding an important contract with a major foreign oil company. The prospects for the reforms supported by the military were further dimmed when Belaúnde's party split in late 1968 and ceased to be a viable reformist alternative for the 1969 elections.

These crises precipitated the coup that brought to power the government of General Juan Velasco Alvarado, one of the most important military reform governments ever to appear in Latin America. Though there are obviously a number of important explanations for the rise to power of this new "military oligarchy," a major one is clearly a concern with self-preservation on the part of the military as an institution in Peruvian society in a period of widespread political crisis and political unrest. In this sense, this fourth period of settlement policy resembles the

95

period of party politics in that policy was shaped to a considerable measure around the interests of political rather than economic groups.

In certain ways, the reforms carried out by this self-proclaimed "revolutionary" government reflect a continuation of the reformist orientation of the military government of 1962 to 1963. However, this earlier concern with reform was greatly intensified by the political crises of the 1960s and by the military's experience of having to use repression to deal with the rural unrest of that period.[2]

The reforms that have been carried out can be seen, in large measure, as having the purpose of eliminating the causes of the crises of the 1960s. One of the most important means through which this is being accomplished is the elimination from the political game of all of the groups that were responsible for the political stalemate of that period. The government has carried out an agrarian reform program that has completed the final liquidation of the traditional elite of the highlands and has destroyed the power of the export oligarchy. Through the elimination of the Congress and the suspension of elections at all but the most local level and through adopting many of the programs long proposed by Apra, Apra has been neutralized, but not repressed. New forms of communitarian economic organization are being introduced in all sectors of the economy, which are intended, in part, to further erode Apra's base of power in the labor movement, as well as to weaken other labor groups that represent a potential threat to the government. Worker participation in industrial communities and in agricultural cooperatives is being introduced as a substitute for the traditional conflict-oriented pattern of labor relations.

At the same time that there is a strong interest in reform, there has also been an intense concern with controlling political participation and channeling political support in ways that are constructive, rather than disruptive, for the government. The experience of the rural land invasions and guerrilla movement of the 1960s and the fear of an urban guerrilla movement have led to a strong emphasis on internal security.

Finally, the policy failures, corruption, and scandals of the Belaúnde period produced a strong concern with ending corruption, with ending a Peruvian tradition of grandiose, unfulfilled government promises, and with restoring respect for law in Peru. There has been a substantial concern with property law, in part because the rural instability of the highlands involved, to a considerable degree, issues of property, and perhaps in part because of the issues of sovereignty and property involved in the oil contract over which there was a major scandal.

In this context of concern with reform, political control, and law, this government has initiated an interesting series of measures in the area of settlement policy. Taken together, these measures constitute a coherent policy which appears to be one of the more interesting aspects of the government's effort to transform Peruvian society. At the same time, however, the government's program is a curious blend of policies from earlier periods. This chapter explores three phases in the evolution of settlement policy in the 1968–75 period. The initial formulation of policy through early 1971 is first considered. The restructuring of policy after the massive Pamplona invasion and other crises of mass political participation in early 1971 is then analyzed.* A postscript then summarizes the pattern of policy failure that emerged toward the end of the Velasco period.

Settlement Policy before the Pamplona Invasion

The first important steps in the development of settlement policy after the coup of October 1968 were the announcement in early November of an army program of leveling streets in settlements and the formation in early December of a new government office concerned with squatter settlements. The program of leveling streets[3] represented a significant contribution to the physical development of the settlements, and by September 1972 the program had been completed in thirty-three settlements.[4] The army has also made major improvements in the highways that lead out to the settlements, particularly to the north of Lima. These highways usually begin as narrow country roads and are totally inadequate for the heavy traffic that develops as tens of thousands of settlement residents establish houses along them. Hence highway improvements represent a major benefit for settlement residents.

On 3 December 1968, the government announced the formation of the Organismo Nacional de Desarrollo de Pueblos Jóvenes, the National Organization for the Development of Young Towns, later known as ONDEPJOV.[5] The importance given to ONDEPJOV was reflected in the fact that it was directly responsible to the president and the prime minister. The most visible innovation that accompanied the founding of ONDEPJOV was the introduction of a new name for settlements—*pueblos jóvenes,* or young towns. An ONDEPJOV publication later suggested that the new term was intended to reflect the recent formation of the

*Though portions of the discussion of this period are in the present or present perfect tense, it will be clear from the postscript to this chapter that this phase of policy had, by 1974–75, been largely superseded.

settlements, the youth of the settlement population, and the residents' desire for community improvement.[6]

The Role of Self-Help

The supreme decree that established ONDEPJOV discussed in detail the positive features of settlements, emphasizing the way in which settlement residents confront their problems of substandard living conditions through self-help. It suggested that the settlement residents had accomplished a great deal with little support from the state, and that if this local initiative were encouraged and directed, even better results could be achieved.[7] The most important aspect of this encouragement has been ONDEPJOV's vigorous effort to build and strengthen community organization in the settlements through training local leaders and encouraging the development of local organizations structured around a series of hierarchically ordered units that reach down to the block level.[8]

The announcement of the members of the executive committee of ONDEPJOV a week after its formation provided further evidence regarding its orientation.[9] One of the most prominent members was the Auxiliary Bishop of Lima, Monseñor Luis Bambarén, who had the title of "Bishop of the Squatter Settlements." Bambarén was strongly identified with the self-help approach. Another member was Diego Robles, an architect with long experience in settlements and author of an article about opportunities for self-help in settlements.[10] The executive committee also included three representatives from the settlements, all of whom were leaders in community organizations involved in self-help projects.

Another important figure in early settlement policy, Carlos Delgado, was not a member of the executive committee. Previously a prominent member of Apra, Delgado quickly emerged as an important advisor to the president at the beginning of the period of military rule. Delgado, like Robles, was the author of an article dealing with self-help development in settlements[11] and had worked in the period before the coup in a government planning office, PLANDEMET, with several people who were later involved in ONDEPJOV, including Robles. There is a striking similarity between the policy recommendations at the end of Delgado's article and the policies the government has followed.

At the same time that these and other civilians held important positions in ONDEPJOV, military officers played a very dominant role. As of 1970, all of the directors of the four zones of ONDEPJOV in Lima were military officers, as well as twenty of the twenty-one directors of the local ONDEPJOV offices in the provinces.[12] Two private community development organizations also had an important influence. Shortly before the coup, Monseñor Bambarén had established a private Oficina de Pueblos Jóvenes to promote self-help projects in settlements. The new name for settlements was originally proposed by a member of this organization, and the emphasis developed by members of this group on active community organization and self-help played an important part in later policy. Acción Comunitaria del Perú has also played an important role. Acción was founded by Acción International of New York, a community development organization which has initiated private community development programs in several Latin American countries. One of the purposes of these programs is to introduce innovative approaches to community development in the hope that they will be imitated by government policy makers.[13] The Peruvian program is now autonomous, supported by the Peruvian private sector. During the first year of the new government, Acción initiated several pilot projects in settlements based on community self-help which became models for the projects later undertaken by the government. The most important of these involved a savings program established in coordination with a private bank through which settlement communities could accumulate capital for the installation of services, particularly electricity. Members of the ONDEPJOV executive committee followed Acción's efforts with considerable interest, making several visits to its main project in the settlement Pamplona Alta. It should also be noted that all three of the settlement representatives on the ONDEPJOV executive committee had worked either with Acción or with Bambarén's private Pueblos Jóvenes office.

The Role of the Private Sector

The association with Acción was just one aspect of the attempt by ONDEPJOV to increase the role of the private sector in the settlements. There was particular interest in coordinating the activities of the private sector with the self-help efforts of the settlement residents.[14] One of the most important aspects of this effort involved encouraging the arrangement initially tried out by Acción in which savings plans are developed with private banks through which money is accumulated for community projects. An early publication of ONDEPJOV included a large table which suggested the ways in which seventeen different types of projects in settlements could be carried out by coordinating the efforts of different combinations of twenty private and public groups.[15] A massive, 392-page catalogue of public and private institutions that provide services to settlements in Lima, Trujillo, Chimbote, and Arequipa was later prepared for ONDEPJOV by the U.S. Agency for International Development.[16]

This catalogue, like many publications of ONDEPJOV, had on its cover a symbolic triangle representing ONDEPJOV's attempt to coordinate these efforts. In some of the publications that have used the symbol the following statement appears below the triangle: "Only the combination of the public sector, the private sector, and the settlement residents can achieve the objectives of . . . the promotion of the economic development and the social and cultural development of the settlements."[17]

Settlement Residents

How is this concern with the role of the private sector to be explained? If this were a quote from the 1950s, one would assume that it was a statement by Pedro Beltrán. The fact that this government has expropriated many of the agricultural holdings of the sector of the rural economy that Beltrán represents, and yet has adopted housing policies proposed by him, illustrates how difficult it is to place the government on a left-right continuum. This interest in encouraging the private sector in settlements is one illustration of the fact that the government is not really anticapitalist, but rather is opposed to certain types of private capital. It would seem to be particularly well disposed toward the kind of small-scale enterprise that is typical of the construction industry.

An important reason for the government's desire to have the private sector actively involved in settlement development is that it shares with Beltrán a belief that the state is not capable, by itself, of dealing with the problem of housing. It is aware of the consistent failure of civilian governments and political parties of the 1950s and 1960s to fulfill the expectations they raised through sweeping promises of government assistance. In 1968 and 1969, one of the most common words used by settlement residents to describe their treatment by earlier governments and political parties was *engaño* (deception). The present government is trying to create realistic expectations about what the government can and cannot do in aiding the settlements, and is seeking to mobilize all available resources—in the public sector, in the private sector, and in the self-help potential of the settlements—to deal with Lima's housing problem.

Legal Status of Settlements

The government is also concerned about the legal status of the settlements. The question of legality has, of course, been an issue for some time. However, it takes on particular interest under the present government because it is an aspect of its overriding concern with law in general, and property law in particular.

The concern with law appears to stem from a belief that ambiguous law, and especially ambiguous property law, may be a source of political instability. This belief is in part a product of the military's experience in the 1960s with rural land invasions and unrest, which were in considerable measure produced by serious ambiguities in land titles. Many of the land seizures in this period were carried out by peasants frustrated by years of expensive litigation over lands of poorly defined legal status of which they felt they were the rightful owners.[18] The experience of repressing these peasant movements had a strong impact on the armed forces and convinced them that fundamental changes were required.[19] Other events in the 1960s doubtless contributed to the concern with law and authority as well. These included the scandal surrounding a major foreign oil contract in August 1968, also involving a question of property rights, and the smuggling scandals of the late Belaúnde period.

The government's concern with law was emphasized immediately after the coup. Decree Law Number One, issued the day after the government came to power, declared that one of the government's objectives was to "restore the principle of authority" and "respect for law" in Peru.[20] Since then, this concern has been reflected in a number of policy areas, including the reform of the court system carried out by the Consejo Nacional de Justicia, the more vigorous enforcement of tax law, the campaign for the "moralization" of public administration, and the attack on corruption in the national police.[21]

The concern with law is also reflected in policy toward settlements. It was clearly expressed in the decree that founded ONDEPJOV, which stated that it was necessary to deal with the problem of property rights in the settlements in the interest of their security and development.[22] Though the program of granting land titles in established settlements would become even more important after the Pamplona invasion in 1971, it was pursued actively from the beginning of the government, first by the Junta Nacional de la Vivienda, the housing agency that had been responsible for the application of Law 13517 during the Belaúnde period, and then by ONDEPJOV. The legalization has been carried out under the terms of Law 13517, as amended by the laws of 1967 and 1968. Remodeling is therefore not a prerequisite for granting title, and the program can proceed with relative ease.

The government's concern with law is also reflected in the policy toward new squatter invasions. The first two and a half years of military rule saw a lull in invasions in the Lima area. A number of people involved with settlements and squatter invasions were given to understand that the government did not intend to tolerate new invasions. Though there were instances of occupation of new land at the edge of established settlements and one case of a land seizure that resulted from a dispute among members of a housing cooperative, there were no substantial new invasions.

The government's determination to prevent invasions was also reflected outside of Lima in October 1969, when a squatter invasion in Talara which received national publicity was met with a firm reaction. This invasion occurred on the first anniversary of the nationalization of the oil complex there, during a visit by President Velasco. The new settlement was named the Ninth of October in honor of the date of the nationalization; and the invaders claimed to have a patriotic desire to commemorate the occasion, but the government moved firmly against them and cleared the site.[23]

Political Support

Another important aspect of the government's concern with settlements is the desire to use them as a base of political support. Like Odría, and unlike the military junta of 1962–63, this government intends to stay in power for some time and has to concern itself with the problem of legitimating its rule. Early evidence of this interest in using the settlements for political support may be found in a demonstration by settlement residents expressing support for the government's policy toward the United States which occurred in the main plaza in front of the presidential palace, just a week after the founding of ONDEPJOV in 1968. This demonstration was organized by Mayor León Velarde, who was involved in the effort to ease the requirements for granting land titles discussed in the previous chapter and who was also a close associate of President Velasco. However, León Velarde's demonstration was smaller and less successful than expected, perhaps in part because his political rivals, particularly Apristas, made a major effort to discourage settlement residents from participating. It therefore did not have the desired impact, and it was some time before the government again attempted to arrange a demonstration of this type.

Following this demonstration, the most visible attempt to rally support involved periodic visits to settlements by General Armando Artola, the Minister of Interior and member of the cabinet who had the greatest ability to mingle with settlement residents. In light of Odría's role in the settlements, it is noteworthy that Artola's father was a minister in Odría's government.[24] In 1969 Artola made many visits to settlements, often arriving spectacularly in a helicopter and giving away used clothing and *panetones* (a type of sweetened bread), dancing traditional Peruvian dances, and occasionally driving the army road graders which were being used to level the streets in settlements.[25]

Two interesting features of these early attempts to develop support in the settlements were the lack of involvement of President Velasco and the lack of coordination between these attempts and the activities of ONDEP-JOV. The lack of a presidential role may have been related to the fact, which was heavily emphasized in the early period of military rule, that this was a government of the military as an institution and not of the president as an individual.[26] The higher-level officers in the government were surely aware of the massive personal support that Odría generated in settlements, as well as of the attempt by Pérez-Godoy to undermine the institutional character of the 1962–63 military government and establish an independent base of power. In light of these past events, it is understandable that the support-getting activity was carried out almost entirely by Artola. He was the "odd man out" in the cabinet, the subject of much of the criticism of the government which circulated in Lima, and the butt of many of the early jokes about the military regime. Permitting him to play a military populist role in settlements allowed the government to begin to seek popular support in settlements without posing the danger that any member of the government would be able to use this as a major base of personal power. At the same time, however, the fact that Artola's father had been a minister in Odría's government might have suggested that giving him free reign in the settlements would be risky. In 1971 Artola did, in fact, make a brief attempt to establish an independent base of support in the settlements.

The separation of the support-getting activities from the program of ONDEPJOV is also striking. ONDEPJOV did not seek wide publicity for its activities. An early ONDEPJOV bulletin emphasized the need to avoid excessive publicity and instead to focus attention on the task of making ONDEPJOV projects effective as a means of gaining the confidence of the settlement population.[27] The difference between this approach and that of Artola was dramatized in May of 1969 when Monseñor Bambarén, an important member of the ONDEPJOV executive committee referred to earlier, held a press conference in which he criticized Artola, stating that the problems of settlements "cannot be solved by gifts and used clothing," but rather by aiding the settlement residents in building their own houses and helping to provide city services. The headline of an article in *Expreso* which reported the press conference—"Solutions, Not Panetones" (*Soluciones, No Panetones*)—clearly summarized the divergence in approaches.[28] These contending approaches reflected the same differences that earlier existed between the approaches of Odría and Beltrán.

This separation between the government's development program and its support-getting activities continued until the founding of SINAMOS in 1971. León Velarde's demonstration might be cited as an example of the coordination of the two aspects of policy, since it occurred just a week after the founding of ONDEPJOV, giving the impression that the demonstration had been planned in part as an expression of gratitude for the new program. However, since one of the settlement representatives on the ONDEPJOV executive committee was a major political rival of León Velarde's, it would appear that the link between these two events was not close.[29]

The Pamplona Invasion

The government's policy of firmness toward invasions was subjected to a difficult test by the massive Pamplona invasion which occurred in Lima in early May 1971.[30] This invasion began on an area of public land on 29 April, spreading to neighboring areas, both public and private, in a series of invasions that continued until 12 May. Tens of thousands of people participated. The government waited several days to initiate attempts to evict the invaders. A series of clashes then occurred which resulted in injury to many invaders and policemen and one death. In one incident, police fired into a crowd of invaders; in another, the invaders captured a police commander and threatened to kill him. They agreed to spare his life when he promised to persuade the government to desist in its efforts at eviction. In the compromise that was finally reached, the invaders agreed to move to a government-prepared site to form a large settlement called Villa el Salvador. Only a small nucleus of the original invasion group remained in an area of public land which they had occupied in the invasion.

The invasion occurred during a meeting in Lima of the board of governors of the Inter-American Development Bank, an agency which in the past had given extensive loans to Peru to support low-income housing projects. The incident would have been a serious embarrassment to the government in any case, but the spectacle of a confrontation between poor families and police and the implication that Peru was not satisfying the housing needs of its low-income population was particularly embarrassing at that time. Invasions in Lima have commonly been timed to produce a maximum effect, and the timing of this invasion was surely no accident.

Various rumors circulated as to who had planned the invasion. The most plausible version suggests that radical student groups were involved, though some sources hint that support may have come from a faction within the government that wished to dramatize Lima's housing needs and force the government to accelerate its programs in the settlements. It was even suggested that Bambarén or Artola had taken part in planning it. Far more important than the question of who organized the invasion, however, was the massive, spontaneous growth of the invasion once it had begun. This demonstrated dramatically the seriousness of the housing deficit in Lima and the vulnerability of the government in the area of housing policy that results from the fact that poor families can meet their housing needs by simply seizing land. It was clear that the slow pace of expansion of settlements during the first two and a half years of the Velasco government had left many families unable to get lots in a settlement and eager to join an invasion. This shortage of lots was further aggravated by the fact that, in contrast to the period of party politics, the Velasco government had not formed any new *urbanizaciones populares.*

The Pamplona invasion is also of interest because it precipitated a second and final clash between Monseñor Bambarén and General Artola. Artola was identified with the hard line vis-à-vis the invaders, whereas after one of the invaders was killed, Bambarén went to the invasion site and held a mass. Artola then had Bambarén arrested for disturbing the peace. The Church vigorously protested the arrest[31] and Artola countered by arranging a demonstration by settlement residents to express support for his activities in the settlements.[32] Bambarén was released after thirteen hours and Artola was forced to resign on 17 May.[33]

Interpretations of Artola's intentions in this situation differ. Some argue that he deliberately delayed the first attempt to evict the invaders, thereby making it more difficult to evict them. It might be speculated that he hoped to increase his importance in the government when he finally succeeded in evicting them or that he would dramatically choose not to, thereby becoming a hero to the settlement residents. It is difficult to find out which, if either, of these alternative versions is true. In either case, Artola was removed from the picture, bringing to an end his spectacular visits to the settlements.

The Pamplona invasion posed a serious challenge to the government's policy of preventing people from obtaining land by simply seizing it, and the government attempted to emphasize that invasions were not a legitimate means of acquiring land. It was announced that "the government will not expropriate these lands in order to legalize the acts of agitators,"[34] perhaps referring to a 1969 law which had expanded the government's ability to expropriate land for low-income housing projects. It was further declared that "the government is revolutionary, but not disorderly, and does not believe that the people are ignorant of the proper means to obtain land."[35]

SINAMOS and the Strategy of Incorporation

Though the Pamplona invasion by itself represented an important crisis for the government, the first half of 1971 was a period of other crises as well, particularly a series of strikes that brought considerable economic and political disruption. These included violent outbreaks in the sugar cooperatives on the north coast and numerous work stoppages in the mines of the central highlands. The miners' strikes substantially reduced mineral exports, thereby damaging Peru's balance of payments, and were finally ended in late March with the arrest of large numbers of union leaders.[36]

The Founding of SINAMOS

All of these events made it clear that the government needed to increase its ability to deal with the sectors of society capable of mass political action. To help meet this need, the government founded SINA-MOS, the Sistema Nacional de Apoyo a la Movilización Social, or National System for the Support of Social Mobilization. Because SINA-MOS has taken over most government programs in settlements, this organization merits particularly close attention in the present analysis. It should be emphasized at the outset that the SINAMOS program in settlements has not been particularly successful. Nonetheless, SINAMOS is of great importance for the present analysis because the strategy of political incorporation that it is employing contrasts strikingly with the strategies that appeared under earlier governments.

Decree Law 18896 of 22 June 1971, which established SINAMOS, declared that this organization was to act as a link between the government and the people, helping to make government bureaucracies more responsive to the public and helping the population to express its desires to the government.[37] This latter objective would be achieved by actively organizing the Peruvian population as a means of creating links between the population and the government and by "orienting" the participation of the population.[38] Some of the language of the law resembled that which had been used earlier by ONDEPJOV with reference to settlements, particularly Article 5a, which said that SINAMOS should help increase the capacity of the population to promote its own development, with the help of the government.

Squatter settlements represent only one sphere of SINAMOS activity. In addition to absorbing ONDEPJOV, SINAMOS is concerned with cooperatives, agrarian reform, and many other areas as well. However, as the organization of SINAMOS developed, it became clear that settlements occupied a position of special importance. SINAMOS is organized in terms of geographic regions which correspond to groups of departments, the largest of the political and administrative units into which Peru is divided. For instance, the Fourth Region corresponds to the Departments of Lima and Ica, plus the Constitutional Province of Callao. There is one exception to this territorial pattern, however. The Tenth Region of SINAMOS is concerned exclusively with the geographically dispersed settlements of metropolitan Lima, despite the fact that everything else in metropolitan Lima falls within the Fourth Region.[39] Thus, the settlements of Lima were singled out for special attention within the organizational structure of SINAMOS.

The special position of settlements in relation to SINAMOS became even more clear with the promulgation of the Organic Law of SINA-MOS, the Decree Law 19352 of 4 April 1972.[40] The introduction to this law described as its goal the establishment of a basically self-directed (*autogestora*) economy in which the means of production are largely controlled by the workers themselves.[41] Squatter settlements obviously fit this model of control perfectly. Whereas in many areas, such as the expropriated coastal sugar haciendas, SINAMOS must oversee the transfer of control from government supervisors to local cooperatives, the settlements have a well-established practice of *autogestión*. Both in the tradition of local initiative in building houses and community facilities and in the practice of electing community leaders,[42] settlements have long had the organizational characteristics that the government seeks to develop elsewhere. The self-help orientation of the settlements is a model for what the government wishes to develop in other sectors of society.

Control of Political Opposition

Apart from the concern with self-direction and self-help, another basic concern of SINAMOS is with controlling political opposition. The strikes that occurred in the period prior to the founding of SINAMOS, and probably the Pamplona invasion as well, had support from opposition parties, and the government is obviously interested in limiting the power of these parties and in competing with them for support at the local level. Though in some situations SINAMOS has permitted people associated with these parties to take over local associations—in part because it would be too costly to prevent it—the overall purpose is to fill the political space which has been, or might be, occupied by these parties by creating alternative organizations in all sectors of Peruvian society.

The concern with the role of political opposition in squatter settlements has been particularly intense. Peruvians who were well informed about the thinking of the government in the early stages of the planning of settlement policy report that there was great concern with the radical potential of the settlements. The attempts of radical university students to organize the settlements politically and the specter of urban guerrillas in other Latin American countries clearly provided a strong basis for these fears. The concern with radicalization in settlements was apparently expressed frequently by the members of the armed forces who were members of ONDEPJOV in discussions of policy within that organization, and the role of army intelligence in ONDEPJOV and in the settlements themselves has been large. There is considerable surveillance of outsiders who enter the settlements, and individuals known to be affiliated with the political left have on occasion been prevented from visiting them. The systematic organization of settlements down to the block level that was first actively encouraged by ONDEPJOV and later by SINAMOS facilitates political control.

The SINAMOS program in the settlements is closely coordinated with the armed forces in a way that enhances political control. It has already been noted that the armed forces have had a direct role in the settlements since the beginning of the period of military rule through their program of leveling streets. The Organic Law of SINAMOS explicitly reaffirms the role of the armed forces in settlement projects.[43] The links between the armed forces and SINAMOS go much further than this, however. SINAMOS uses the army radio communications system to conduct much of its business in settlements, permitting instantaneous communication among all of the settlement areas surrounding Lima. Three of the five generals who are commanders of the military regions of Peru, the basic units of territorial division of the command structure of the armed forces, are also the heads of the corresponding regions of SINAMOS.[44] In particular, the commander of the Lima Military Region is also head of the Tenth Region of SINAMOS, the one that is concerned exclusively with Lima settlements. It is striking that this commander is in charge of the region that includes only the settlements, and not the region that includes the department as a whole.

Without overstating the importance of the links between the formal structure of the army and the organization of SINAMOS, it is clear that it is related to the government's preoccupation with the potential for radical political activity in the settlements. If an urban guerrilla movement were to develop there, SINAMOS and the army would be in a good position to move quickly against it.

The relationship of SINAMOS with the local leaders in settlements is also a channel of potential control. SINAMOS does not prevent members of political parties from being elected as leaders but will remove them if they act for their party in their leadership role. The only formal requirements for leadership are living in the settlement, being at least eighteen years old and literate, having a known occupation, and having a "good background," that is to say, not having a police record.[45] Having a known occupation does not mean that a leader is excluded if he is temporarily unemployed. Rather, he at some point must have had a regular job. This provision, along with the requirement of residence in the settlement, is intended to exclude professional political organizers. SINAMOS maintains a central archive of records on all leaders.[46] Because SINAMOS has made student political organizing in settlements more difficult, has channeled private programs through the leadership structure that it created in settlements, and is keeping close track of these leaders, it has established a substantial degree of control over the political life of the settlements.

Popular Support

Another important consequence of the formation of SINAMOS has been to bring together in one agency the government's programs in settlements and its attempts to mobilize popular support. These had previously been divided between ONDEPJOV and Artola. SINAMOS has arranged major demonstrations by settlement residents, such as the demonstration in Chimbote on 29 July 1972, the day after the national Independence Day, which a SINAMOS bulletin claimed was attended by 120,000 people.[47] SINAMOS literature on Villa el Salvador likewise focuses on popular support. An article on this settlement in *SINAMOS Informa*, a news bulletin put out by SINAMOS, included eight pictures of residents of Villa el Salvador engaged in large, enthusiastic demonstrations, waving Peruvian flags and banners which carried slogans supporting the government.[48] SINAMOS regularly organizes settlement residents for demonstrations on national holidays and other occasions, thus following an important precedent from the Odría period.

President Velasco developed a close relationship with Villa el Salvador, and he and particularly his wife made a number of personal visits to the settlement.[49] This departed from Velasco's initial practice of not being personally identified with settlement programs. Thus Velasco, like Odría and Beltrán before him, finally had his own settlement and his own base of popular support.

There is a significant divergence between the reality of the political demonstrations arranged by SINAMOS and the officially stated objectives of SINAMOS of supporting "mobilization." The law that founded SINAMOS declares that one of its purposes is to create a dialogue between the people and the government and to stimulate the participation of the people in basic decisions.[50] The publicity regarding these demonstrations claims that they fulfill these purposes. On various occasions, settlement residents or members of other groups attending the demonstrations have been brought up to the platform to make a statement about their needs. This is referred to in the publicity as "dialogue."[51] Similarly, SINAMOS publicity regarding the July 1972 settlement demonstration in Chimbote stated that demonstrations of this type are a "consequence of a coherent policy which is intended to encourage the participation of the citizenry in the tasks of development and progress."[52] The claims of SINAMOS regarding the significance of these demonstrations were also reflected in the main banner that hung below the speaker's platform at the Chimbote demonstration, which said *"Tu Presencia es Revolución"* ("Your Presence is Revolution").[53]

These demonstrations may reflect considerable support for the government. However, mass involvement in this kind of dialogue, participation, and "revolution" does not really involve the exercise of political power. The emphasis on this type of symbolic participation reflects a basic dilemma of military governments, even reformist or radical military governments, regarding the appropriate role of mass participation. The typical solution to this dilemma is nicely summarized by Stepan, who suggests that "in regard to participation, the desire of military radicals for control would tend to conflict with free democratic electoral campaigns, but would be congruent with a military populist plebiscitary style of politics. As regards mobilization, military radicals' preference for order and unity would make them . . . favorably disposed to mass parades."[54] Hence, in spite of the many ways in which the policies of this government differ from those of the Odría period, there is a striking continuity in the concern with this plebiscitary use of popular support in settlements.

At the same time, however, the participation that is being encouraged in settlements by SINAMOS does affect decision making at the local level. Local associations are democratic and, within the limitations imposed on local political activity, settlement residents do exercise choice in decisions about local development programs. It is in considerable measure through its extensive efforts to develop this participation at the local level—and the impressive results that have been achieved so far through these efforts—that the program of the present government departs sharply from that of Odría.

Summing up the changes in settlement policy that resulted from the Pamplona invasion and the other crises of mass participation that occurred at about the same time, it is clear that two basic goals of the policy—promoting development based on self-help and gaining political support—remained unaltered. However, whereas previously these two goals were pursued separately by ONDEPJOV and Artola, the consequence of the political crisis was to bring them together in SINAMOS in such a way as to strengthen a third element—the capacity for political control. Though the concern with political control was present from the beginning, it was heightened by the crises of early 1971. This is yet another example of the way in which crises of mass participation have produced a restructuring of mechanisms of political control in Peru.

Settlement Policy, Law, and Urbanization after the Pamplona Invasion

Apart from the strategy of incorporation, other aspects of policy have crystalized since the Pamplona invasion, including development policy in settlements, policy toward law and property in the settlements, and the relation of settlement policy to urbanization.

Development Policy in Settlements

Since the Pamplona invasion, the government's development programs in settlements have become more extensive and visible, if for no other reason than the massive scale of the program in Villa el Salvador, the government-sponsored settlement formed to accommodate the families who participated in the Pamplona invasion. The government is attempting to develop the settlement through the prompt installation of city services and provision of land titles. The residents may build their own houses or select one of several models of prefabricated houses which are manufactured by the private sector and which are on display in the settlement.

The government's long-run goal is to turn Villa el Salvador into what was initially referred to as a *Ciudad Cooperativa* (Cooperative City) and which by 1974 was usually referred to as the world's first *Comunidad Urbana Autogestionaria* (Self-Managing Urban Community). This settlement, which by 1974 had a population of between 125,000 and 150,000, was divided into hundreds of local committees in which dozens of organizers trained in the methods of forming cooperatives were working.[55] The goal is to develop a community that will deal not only with the need for housing and city services but also with more basic problems of employment. A settlement of this size includes workers from a wide variety of occupations, and the goal is to bring them together in a cooperative that would sell goods and services to the community. To facilitate this, a large area of land close to the community was left unoccupied to provide space for the development of various types of light manufacturing. During the Belaúnde period, land was similarly put aside near a government-sponsored settlement, but this land was later filled with new settlements. One important indicator of the commitment of the present government to preventing uncontrolled invasions and to promoting the economic self-sufficiency of Villa el Salvador will be whether it succeeds in keeping this reserved land available for its intended use. The privileged position of Villa el Salvador among the government's development goals is reflected by the fact that it was the first community in greater Lima to be serviced by a new type of oversized express buses which were introduced in mid-1974. These buses both greatly facilitated commuting to the central areas of the city and gave a special prestige to Villa el Salvador.

Though the level and scale of government activity is lower in other settlements, SINAMOS is actively involved in many other areas as well, promoting the formation of cooperatives for housing and the installation of services. The much stronger framework of community organization which ONDEPJOV and SINAMOS have built in the settlements is an important factor in projects such as the installation of water pipes which are based in part on labor contributed by the residents themselves. Each household is expected to contribute labor to these projects. If a household does not contribute labor and likewise fails to make a financial contribution equivalent to the estimated value of its labor, it will not receive the service. In order to accumulate capital for the acquisition of services, savings schemes have been established with the cooperation of private banks through which funds are accumulated. SINAMOS emphasizes that its role is not one of providing for all of the needs of settlements, but rather of coordinating the efforts of the residents and the private sector in promoting settlement development.

Concern with Law

Another important aspect of policy after the Pamplona invasion involves the government's concern with law. This has been expressed most importantly in policy toward new invasions and toward legalization.

New Invasions. The basic pattern followed in dealing with the Pamplona invasion has been applied to other invasions as well. For instance, in the case of a small invasion of an archaeological site outside of Lima in 1972, negotiations between SINAMOS and the invaders resulted in an agreement that the invaders would move to land at the edge of an already established settlement.[56] On the other hand, the government has been unable to enforce this pattern in the case of four invasions which occurred along the Rimac River to the west of the center of Lima in October of 1972, timed to coincide with the fourth anniversary of the military coup.[57] Though SINAMOS was able to move two of the groups to other sites within the same immediate area, it has been unable to persuade the invaders to move to Villa el Salvador. Even police efforts to prevent further growth of these settlements produced some violence,[58] and the government has been unwilling to apply the degree of violence that would be necessary to remove the invaders from the sites. In part in response to the failure to deal successfully with these invasions, the government promulgated Decree Law 20066 of 26 June 1973, which made involvement in invasions punishable by imprisonment of up to two years. This punishment applied not only to those who actually participated in invasions, but also anyone involved in organizing an invasion.[59] SINAMOS has also tried to penalize the squatters who refused to move to Villa el Salvador by delaying the registration of lots in these settlements in a way that seriously inhibits investment and self-help efforts on the part of the residents.

This apparent firmness of the policy toward invasions should not obscure important failures and limitations in the government's policy. For one thing, the rate at which squatters are occupying individual plots at the edge of already established settlements has been sufficiently high as to neutralize the effect of the policy of controlling invasions in terms of the overall rate of settlement growth. In addition, all of the evictions in Lima during the early Velasco period were in response to invasions that occurred on private land. The initial invasion group in the Pamplona invasion of 1971, which occupied public land, was never evicted. The invasions in provincial cities referred to above which resulted in evictions also occurred on private land. It was shown in Chapter III that most governments have reacted firmly to invasions of private land. Hence one must not overstate the degree to which the reaction of the Velasco government is distinctive, since it may instead be the pattern of invasions that is distinctive.

How can this pattern of invasions of private land be explained? To the extent that the invasions are being planned by opposition parties or student groups, it may be that this is part of a strategy of harassing the government by forcing it again and again to evict invaders, creating a spectacle of disorder that is obviously distasteful to the government. These invasions may also be viewed as a ritual in which would-be squatters invade private land in order to get moved to public land by the government. A final factor may be the growing shortage of desirable public land to invade that is a reasonable distance from the center of Lima. By invading private land, the invasion groups of October 1972 were able to force SINAMOS to find them land at a more convenient distance from the city.

Legalization. SINAMOS is actively granting land titles in settlements, and in 1972 was processing tens of thousands of applications for titles. Many more titles were granted from 1970 to 1972 than throughout the 1960s.[60] An interesting aspect of this program of legalization concerns the requirements imposed for applying for a land title in a settlement. Among the documents that SINAMOS requires is a certificate of civil marriage.[61] This is a particularly significant requirement since many couples in settlements are joined only by common-law marriage. Though it is possible to make the application without the certificate, the belief that it will be required has produced a rash of mass marriages in settlements.[62] For conservatives who view the tradition of common-law marriages among cityward migrants and rural Indians as a sign of national backwardness, the newly legalized marriages are doubtless a source of great satisfaction. This is another way in which the government is extending the rule of law to the settlements.

SINAMOS is also attempting to force settlement residents to occupy the lots of which they claim to be the de facto owners, or to give them up. The need to do this arises from the fact that many families have treated squatter invasions as an opportunity for land speculation, initially occupying a lot in a new settlement and building a minimal house on it, but not living there. This is done with the intention of moving in later on, or renting or selling the house and lot at some future date. Law 13517 prohibits this, and housing agencies have tried, usually unsuccessfully, to prevent it. In September of 1972 SINAMOS began a major effort to end this practice.[63] Though obviously confronted by many of the same difficulties that earlier agencies faced in enforcing this aspect of the law, SINAMOS had a greater ability to recover the unused lots because of its extensive efforts to organize the settlements. The local settlement organizations collect contributions from the residents for community projects, and to the extent that lots are not occupied, the ability to collect money is correspondingly reduced. SINAMOS therefore expected full cooperation from the settlement leaders in their campaign. However, as with many aspects of the SINAMOS program, it appears that the effort to recover lots has met with, at best, only modest success.

New Settlements and Policy toward Urbanization

Fully as significant as the firm policy toward invasions is the fact that, apart from Villa el Salvador, the government is not making use of the provisions of Law 13517 that allow it to form new *urbanizaciones populares*. This is an important change in policy from the period of party politics. Interviews with SINAMOS officials revealed that there does exist, however, a legal means through which families can acquire a lot in a settlement. This *via legal* involves a program in which lots in government-sponsored settlements are sold to any family that applies for one. However, out of fear of stimulating a massive demand for new lots, this program has received little publicity and hence has operated only on a small scale. As of 1972, a common way of getting a lot was to participate in an invasion and then get moved to a government-sponsored settlement. Invasions thus continue to be a major means through which families acquire land in settlements. In addition, as was noted above, many other families are acquiring land by simply occupying lots at the edge of existing settlements. This has produced a particularly rapid growth in the settlement population in the vast area of settlements to the south of Lima near Villa el Salvador.

Given the concern with adherence to law, it is surprising that the government tolerates and, by moving invaders to new sites, even provides some incentive for this disorderly pattern of settlement growth. The invasions that are occurring are clearly related to a continuing shortage of low-cost housing in Lima. Though opposition parties or land speculators might still be interested in invasions if this shortage did not exist, the elimination of the shortage would unquestionably remove one of the causes of these invasions. The program of offering lots to any family that applies for one could alleviate the shortage, but the government is reluctant to develop the program sufficiently to allow this to happen.

The reason for this reluctance lies in the overall development strategy of the government. Through efforts to develop other parts of the coast, extensive agrarian reform, and programs to develop the jungle, this government hopes to stem the heavy flow of migration to Lima. In this sense its orientation is similar to that of Belaúnde.[64] A massive program of offering land in settlements to any family that applied for it would make life in Lima easier for new migrants and would be a stimulus for new migration to the capital. It appears that the government is willing to tolerate the continuing occurrence of invasions in Lima as a price it must pay for holding down the rate of migration to the capital.

This concern with decentralization has also been reflected in policy toward invasions in the provinces. There have been evictions in provincial cities.[65] However, the reaction to invasions has been far less harsh outside of Lima. It appears that there has been a deliberate strategy of restraining invasions in Lima and letting them occur more freely in provincial cities. This is intended to discourage migration to Lima, and to encourage instead the concentration of migrants in secondary population centers.[66] Concern with legality thus once again takes second place to the concern with restraining migration to Lima.

Though the efforts to restrain invasions in Lima and the greater tolerance for invasions in the provinces are consistent with a policy of decentralization, the massive growth of Villa el Salvador would, by itself, appear to have canceled out any beneficial effects that might have resulted from these other aspects of the policy. There is an important sense in which this is not the case, however. If one characterizes the significance of Villa el Salvador in terms of alternative urban development strategies, it becomes clear that it involves not so much a stimulus to the further growth of Lima as an attempt to form a satellite city. To the extent that the effort to provide employment within the settlement is successful, it will become economically autonomous. Earlier settlements have been primarily residential communities, though some businesses, particularly small shops, have appeared in them. They have relied on Lima as their principal source of employment, and hence add to the demand for employment in Lima. To the extent that significant centers of employment do develop in Villa el Salvador, it will have the effect of decentralizing the demand for employment. Hence, the policy toward Villa el Salvador is more nearly consistent with the government's overall development strategy.

Urban Reform

A useful means of characterizing current policy is to examine not only the policies that have been adopted but also those that have been rejected. Urban reform represents an important policy alternative which has been widely discussed in Lima under the Velasco government but which has not been adopted. Ever since the Cuban urban reform of 1960, reform governments in Latin America have had a model for the fundamental rearrangement of the ownership of urban property. The Cuban law eliminated renting, put all home construction in the hands of the state, imposed new norms for the inheritance of real estate, and placed future urban expansion under tight government control.[67]

The Cuban law was printed in Lima and circulated widely in the first years of military rule.[68] Support for urban reform came from the political left: from the magazine *Oiga* during the first year of military rule when it was to the left of the government; from the most reform-minded members of the government, both civilian and military; and, more recently, from the Christian Democratic party, which has close ties to the government.[69] The proposals of *Oiga* and the Christian Democrats included the expropriation of rented housing. In one version, back rent would have counted as partial payment toward purchase, and the government would have paid the balance.[70] This would not necessarily have involved all rented housing, and *Oiga* suggested that small-scale owners who were renting only two or three properties should be exempted.[71] The reform would also have curbed land speculation in areas of future urban expansion at the periphery of the city—an important factor in housing costs—through expropriation of areas of future urban growth and more careful planning of city growth.[72]

President Velasco's Independence Day speech on 28 July 1969 emphatically ruled out the possibility of a general redistribution of urban real estate but made it clear that some control over land speculation was imminent.[73] He declared that there would not be urban reform, as some had "self-interestedly" maintained (in part a slap at *Oiga*), and that the government would not eliminate the right to private property in the form of real estate, but rather would defend it. Instead, the concern of the government was with resolving the problems of squatter settlements and inner-city slums and with eliminating land speculation. He was particularly forceful on this last point, declaring that "We all know that in Peru, immense fortunes have been made through artificially driving up the price of . . . land. . . . This is a situation of appalling injustice which cannot continue in the future."[74]

This speech naturally raised wide expectations of new measures dealing with settlements and slums and with land speculation. Endless rumors circulated about a new squatter settlement law. According to one version the law would attack the problems of inner-city slums by offering new land to the slum residents and then eradicating the slums.[75] Another version suggested the law involved cooperative ownership of settlements by the residents which would preclude individual ownership of houses. A law based on this latter idea was apparently drafted and circulated in the government, but was never approved. Hence, settlement policy continued to be carried out under the terms of Law 13517, as revised in the late Belaúnde period.

On the other hand, Law 17803, dealing with land speculation, came out a little over a month after Velasco's speech.[76] This law provided the basis for expropriating land for use in low-income housing developments and included fairly strict criteria for determining the price of expropriation and the terms of payment to the owners. The measure was generally well received, with some complaints from private developers about the terms of expropriation.[77] However, to the author's knowledge, no significant use has been made of the law.

Why was urban reform not adopted? The parallel with agrarian reform was inviting. In rural areas, land invasions had threatened the stability of the system and land was being redistributed to preempt future invasions. In urban areas, land seizures continued to occur, and it would seem reasonable to preempt them through the redistribution of urban property. However, there were major differences. Redistribution in the capital might conflict with the government's goal of diverting migration from Lima, whereas redistribution in rural areas was obviously consistent with it. Likewise, agrarian reform in the highlands took land from a class of traditional hacienda owners whose political power had long been declining. In urban areas, the private sector played an important role in the government's housing plans, and the government perhaps did not wish to demoralize this sector by carrying out extensive expropriations. Other factors may have been influential as well, such as the fact that the government did not want to inhibit private investment in housing with a threatening law and that some high-ranking military officers own significant amounts of urban real estate. In spite of these various reasons for thinking that an urban reform is unlikely, it continues to be discussed in Lima, and as of mid-1974 some observers thought that such a reform might still be carried out.

With regard to the possibility of new, comprehensive legislation for settlements and slums, the proposal for cooperative ownership of settlements was viewed in the cabinet and elsewhere as undermining the principle of private property, and hence was dropped. Because settlements make property owners out of the urban poor, a feature of settlements that has often been viewed as contributing to political stability, the government was apparently reluctant to eliminate this aspect of settlement life. The reasons why the massive relocation of slum residents was not carried out are less clear. If the old slum areas were eradicated, there was no reason why this measure should have stimulated further migration to Lima. It might also have helped to reduce the number and size of the squatter invasions that were occurring in Lima. On the other hand, it would have represented a major assault on private control of urban real estate. It would also have committed the government to a massive task of demolishing old slums and of aiding new communities at the periphery of the city. Finally, in light of the failures of the Belaúnde period, the government has been reluctant to get committed to programs that it may not be able to complete. This particular program may have appeared to require a larger commitment than the government felt it was wise to make.

Placing current policy in the context of alternative policies which have not been adopted helps to bring into focus the overall development strategy of the government. In avoiding the kind of policy commitments involved in Law 13517, the government has rejected with reference to settlement policy what Anderson has called the "democratic reform" approach, based on sweeping policy commitments and a large role of the public sector.[78] In rejecting the alternative of a basic reordering of urban property relationships, it has also rejected, with reference to settlement policy, what Anderson calls the "revolutionary" approach, which views the existing modern sector as an obstacle to development.[79] Instead, the policy for developing the settlements that has been adopted falls within the "conventional" approach, based on an elaboration of the contribution of the existing private sector—as well, of course, as the potential for self-help that exists within the settlements themselves.[80] In this sense, in terms of Anderson's categories, the government is far from revolutionary.

Comparisons with Other Governments

The policies toward settlements adopted by the present military government appear to be guided by a number of concerns: a desire to avoid commitments to programs that are so comprehensive and require such extensive resources that they cannot be carried out; the desire to avoid programs that further encourage the growth of Lima; the desire to reconstruct Peruvian society around partially autonomous units which operate on the basis of *autogestión*, or self-direction; and the attempt to promote a particular type of popular support and controlled mass participation which is unrelated to political demand making, except for demands focused at the local level, and which precludes the traditional political parties. Though the government must occasionally choose from among these goals—as in the choice between respect for law and controlling urban growth, they form overall the basis for a fairly coherent and consistent policy.

An examination of the precedents for current policy reveals a curious blend of policies pursued by an earlier progressive government and by the political right. Odría's use of settlements as a base of popular support and as part of his campaign against Apra anticipated current activities of SINAMOS. Beltrán's emphasis on self-help and on the role of the private sector in solving the housing crisis has been revived. Belaúnde's concern with the impact of massive settlement programs on urban growth is also reflected in the present period.

It would, however, be a mistake to argue that the government is merely applying old policies. Even if many aspects of the policy have been tried out under earlier governments, it is an innovation to bring the different aspects of the policy together. Belaúnde attempted to shift development priorities to rural areas, but in the process totally neglected the settlements and failed to curb their extremely rapid growth in the 1960s. The present government, by contrast, is attempting to divert migration *at the same time* that it aids settlements. Likewise, Odría appears to have maintained political control in part by neglecting legalization, presumably at great cost to the settlement residents. The present government is attempting to control the political life of the settlements *at the same time* that it is granting land titles.

This difference between the Odría and Velasco periods merits close attention. It was argued in Chapter IV that Odría established a relationship with the poor based on dependence in which the informality of policy appeared to enhance political control. The present government, by contrast, is relying on a system of control based on an attempt to systematically structure and penetrate community organizations in the settlements. By channeling all aid programs, public and private, through this organizational structure, SINAMOS has attempted to fill the political space in the settlements, drastically reducing the number of alternative courses of political action open to settlement residents. The high degree of power asymmetry that existed under Odría is still present, but the informality of the system is not. Indeed, one of the most important features of the organizational system set up by SINAMOS is that it is consistent and predictable. Following the current usage of the term, this system of control may properly be called corporative.[81] As such, it represents a third distinct type of authoritarian rule that has been reflected in settlement policy in Lima.

Changing Definitions of Benefits and Costs

A useful means of summarizing the changes in settlement policy that have occurred under the Velasco government is to return to the idea of settlement policy as a "distributive" policy, which was presented at the end of Chapter III. It was suggested that the highly informal policy of permitting the appropriation of land corresponded clearly to a broad category of public policies which Lowi has called distributive. A crucial feature of these policies is that they involve a policy arena in which there are no well-defined losers. In the case of settlement policy, this was possible because the wealthy as well as the poor could benefit from the policy and because the thing that was being acquired as a result of the policy—land—was highly divisible. It was therefore relatively easy to offer payoffs to all contenders and to create a political game in which there appeared to be no losers.

From this perspective, it may be suggested that recent changes in settlement policy have come in large measure because of a change in the political context which caused the government to conclude that settlement formation was more costly than had previously been realized—that it was a game in which there were, indeed, losers. One aspect of the change in context was the rural instability in the Peruvian highlands in the 1960s and the link between this instability and ambiguous property law. The military apparently concluded that the ambiguous system of property law had already imposed a high cost by threatening the stability of the system in rural areas and that it might do so in urban areas as well. The military government has therefore been attempting to bring order to the system of property law, in urban as well as rural areas.

Though the military fears the radical potential of the settlements, this presumed radical potential has not, in fact, yet produced significant political disruption in Lima. The disruption occurred, instead, in the countryside. Following Hirschman, it may be argued that this is an instance in which a "neglected" problem—the landholding arrangements in Lima—received attention in part because its solution is viewed as an aspect of the solution of a "privileged" problem—the landholding arrangements in rural areas.[82]

Other changes in the political context were important as well. The idea that settlement formation imposes a high cost by encouraging migration to Lima had already influenced policy in earlier periods. The specter of urban guerrillas in other countries also affected the military's perceptions of the costs of uncontrolled settlement formation in Lima. Still another change that has affected the costs of settlement formation has been the decreasing availability of unused land within a reasonable distance of the center of Lima. Though the improvement of highways can have the effect of making distant land more accessible or the development of Villa el Salvador as a satellite city can make the issue of closeness to Lima less relevant, it appears that the declining availability of land has had an important influence on policy. This has obviously altered one of the conditions for the operation of the earlier policy—the fact that there was always more land available a bit farther down the road. The non–zero sum character of the earlier policy has clearly been undermined by this change in the pattern of availability of land.

These changing patterns of costs and benefits of settlement formation and the decreasing availability of land have caused a shift from a distributive, giveaway policy to a policy of attempting to regulate land use. This regulation includes not only the attempt to control settlement formation, but also Law 17803, which laid the basis for regulating land speculation. The shift has resulted in considerable measure from the identification of new interests—the requirements of a particular national development strategy and the presumed requirements of national security—which are now perceived as having been jeopardized by the earlier policy.

This pattern of evolution from distributive to regulative is not unique to settlement policy in Peru. Lowi has observed a similar pattern of evolution in the case of tariff policy in the United States and has also explained this evolution in terms of changes in the broader political context in which the policy exists.

Lowi suggests that in the earlier part of this century in the United States, most strikingly with the Smoot-Hawley Tariff of 1930, United States tariff policy was based on "thousands of obscure decisions [which] merely accumulated into a policy of protection. . . ."[83] Congress sought support by "giving limited protection (indulgence) to all interests strong enough to furnish resistance."[84] It involved a situation in which "a billion dollar issue [could] be disaggregated into many millions of nickel-dime items and each [could] be dealt with without regard to the others. . . ."[85]

Beginning in the 1930s, however,

> the tariff began to lose its capacity for infinite disaggregation because it slowly underwent redefinition, moving away from its purely domestic significance towards that of an instrument of international politics. In brief, the tariff, especially following World War II and our assumption of peacetime international leadership, became a means of regulating the domestic economy for international purposes. The significant feature here is not the international but the regulatory part of the redefinition. As the process of redefinition took place, a number of significant shifts in power relations took place as well, because it was no longer possible to deal with each dutiable item in isolation. . . . Certain elements of distributive politics remain . . . [because] there are always efforts to disaggregate policies as the best way to spread the patronage and to avoid conflict. . . . But despite the persistence of certain distributive features, the true nature of tariff in the 1960's emerges as a regulatory policy.[86]

Thus with tariff policy in the United States, as with settlement policy in Peru, new, broader interests emerged that could not be served by the earlier distributive pattern. In both cases, changing elite perceptions of the costs and benefits associated with the particular areas of policy were a major force in producing policy change.

Postscript: The End of the Velasco Period

Since this chapter was written, it has become increasingly evident that the settlement policies of the Velasco period had been seriously eroded by important failures during roughly the last two years of the Velasco presidency, which ended in August 1975.[87] The policy of containing settlement growth was unsuccessful. Neither Villa el Salvador nor the *vía legal* had adequately relieved the pressure for new lots, and exceptionally rapid growth continued as tens of thousands of new squatters occupied land at the edges of already established settlements.

SINAMOS also failed to achieve other important goals in the settlements. Because it lacked adequately experienced personnel, did not follow through on projects it had helped to initiate, and had a perhaps excessive concern with using its access to the settlement population as a means of mobilizing political support, rather than effectively helping the settlements, SINAMOS increasingly antagonized large numbers of settlement residents. Although physical development in many settlements—including Villa el Salvador and a number of settlements in which the granting of land titles advanced rapidly—was impressive, these other failures undermined the position of SINAMOS in settlements. The attempt to penalize the residents of the settlements formed in the October 1972 invasions by withholding support for the development of these communities backfired: the residents became militantly antagonistic toward SINAMOS, eventually setting fire to the SINAMOS headquarters for their area of Lima. There appeared to be declining confidence in the ability of SINAMOS to maintain effective political control through the organizational network that it had established and also a growing reliance on direct police involvement in the settlements. Though there had been some presence of the Policía de Investigación (the equivalent of the F.B.I.) in the settlements from the beginning of the Velasco period, the years after the Pamplona invasion brought a significant increase in police surveillance of the settlements.

These failures of settlement policy do not, of course, reduce the importance of the Velasco period from the perspective of the present analysis. The concern of this book has been with assessing the changing approaches to settlement policy that have emerged out of a series of distinct political crises, and the examination of the Velasco period has made it possible to carry this assessment a step further. These recent developments do, however, serve as a useful reminder concerning the importance of policy failure under authoritarian regimes. Because authoritarian regimes often come to power in response to policy failure under democratic regimes, it is at times too easy to overlook the degree to which they are themselves vulnerable to policy failure. While it is analytically useful to classify these regimes as authoritarian, it must be remembered that in many areas of policy they may be dramatically unsuccessful in exercising authority.

VIII

Policy Change in
Comparative Perspective

This book began with a simple question: how is it possible that in a country that has been as oligarchic and authoritarian as Peru there could be such a massive growth of squatter settlements around the nation's capital? Contrary to the assumptions or conclusions of much previous research, it appears that the growth of settlements in Lima has been in part the result of the covert, and at times overt, support of the Peruvian state and the Peruvian elite.

This support has been extended for a variety of reasons. It has served in part as an inexpensive form of aid to the urban poor, as a means of facilitating evictions from inner-city slums, and as a means of gaining political support. Policy toward settlement formation has also been linked to policy regarding urbanization, agrarian reform, and the protection of property. Because settlement formation appears to encourage urbanization, there has been an inverse relation between each government's interest in limiting urbanization and in encouraging settlement formation. Because urbanization appears to serve as a safety valve in rural areas, perhaps making it easier to postpone such forms of rural change as agrarian reform, there has been an inverse relation between the degree of commitment of each government to agrarian reform and its willingness to encourage settlement formation. Because settlement formation is an important aspect of the ambiguity of Peru's system of property law, governments interested in ending ambiguities of law and disrespect for law have tried to discourage settlement formation and to actively promote the legalization of existing settlements. Finally, policy toward settlement formation and toward the subsequent development of settlements has been deliberately used to shape and control political expression in the settlements. Because this is the case, the analysis of settlement policy has provided an opportunity for exploring the evolving approaches to limiting political pluralism that have emerged in Peru—and hence an opportunity for examining the emergence of distinct subtypes of authoritarian rule and the relationship between these subtypes and the overall process of modernization.

Settlement Policy and Authoritarian Rule

In order to bring this relationship between economic and social modernization and the emergence of distinct subtypes of authoritarian rule into focus, it is appropriate at this point to review the findings regarding a series of linked issues that were raised in the first chapter: the relation between the process of modernization, the emergence of new political groups, political crises, changing political coalitions, and policy change; evolving patterns of limitation of pluralism and subtypes of authoritarian rule; and changes in patterns of political control and in the autonomy of the political sphere.

Modernization, Political Groups, Crises, Coalitions, and Policy Change

A basic argument of this book is that the forces that have brought changes in settlement policy can ultimately be traced back to certain fundamental modernizing transformations that have occurred in Peruvian society in the twentieth century: the emergence of an export economy based on enclave development; the pattern of economic and social displacement which it produced; and a number of other changes in the occupational and social structure of Peru in both rural and urban areas. These processes of modernization created a series of new political actors—the export elite, the Apra party, and other new parties that had a major base in urban areas. The stalemate and political crises produced by the interaction of these new groups in turn helped to stimulate important transformations in the Peruvian military such that, by the late 1960s, the military itself had been converted into a new kind of actor in the Peruvian political system.

The rising power of these new groups produced a succession of distinct economic and political interests which came to shape settlement policy. In the first period considered, the need of the export elite and the military to protect themselves in the face of the crisis produced by the attempted incorporation of Apra into the electoral system in the mid-1940s—combined with the personal ambition of Odría—produced Odría's coup and the onset of the first period of settlement policy. It was also noted that there was a striking congruence between the form of elite-mass relations promoted through settlement policy in this period and that which characterized the traditional, semifeudal haciendas of the Peruvian highlands. Because Odría had certain important links with this traditional sector, it seemed possible that the haciendas of the highlands had provided a model for the relationship that he was promoting with the settlements. This pattern of elite-mass relations in the broader society and in the settlements represented a kind of "base line" from which there was subsequently a clear evolution in both spheres.

In the second or liberal period, the economic interests of one of the principal groups spun out of Peru's process of modernization—the export elite and associated urban commercial interests—directly shaped settlement policy. The classical liberalism of this sector, which is reflected in its support for private enterprise, a small role for the state in society, and laissez-faire economic policies, led directly to the particular approach to settlements that was adopted by Beltrán.

The third period of settlement policy was shaped by another new type of political actor which grew out of the process of modernization—political parties. It was argued that parties are a distinctive type of political organization whose need for mass electoral support inclines them toward an approach to public policy that is oriented toward sweeping policy commitments and is totally distinct from the approach of the liberal period. The nature of these distinct needs of parties was summarized by the observation that "Teach the poor to take care of themselves," a phrase that might be used to summarize the liberal approach, hardly makes a good electoral slogan in a country in which the mass of the population is poor.

Finally, from 1968 to 1975, policy was shaped by a military government that sought to resolve the political crises of the 1960s, which were produced in considerable measure by the political stalemate and failure of reform of the Belaúnde period.

It is evident from the preceding discussion that recurring political crises are an important intervening variable between the appearance of the new economic and political groups that have emerged out of the process of modernization and policy change. The political crises of the 1940s were directly responsible for Odría's rise to power. When Odría's policies began to take directions that threatened the interests of the export oligarchy, Beltrán introduced his own approach to settlements, which was intended to serve both as a source of political support in his battle with Odría and as an alternative solution to the crisis of political mobilization posed by Apra. The crises of the 1960s brought the Velasco government to power and played a central role in shaping settlement policy. Finally, the Pamplona invasion and the crises of mass mobilization of early to mid-1971 were responsible for an important shift in the way in which policy was carried out, if not in its substance. Political crises have thus played a central role in influencing the patterns of authoritarian rule that have been reflected in settlement policy. It is hardly a surprising finding that political crises should produce policy change. However, it is only recently that crises have begun to be treated in a systematic way as a focus of political analysis.[1]

This context of modernization and the political crises and evolving political coalitions that emerged from it is, of course, not the only source of policy change. Another source of change is to be found in the inner logic of settlements as an issue area. It was argued that once the Peruvian government had actively begun to encourage the formation of settlements, a "sorcerer's apprentice dynamic" was set up in which, for the already established settlements, the informal giving away of land of the kind that had occurred under Odría was simply not sufficient and a broad range of new forms of aid and assistance to the settlement residents had to be invented. The gradual evolution of policy in such areas as the granting of land titles may be interpreted in part as resulting from the continuing need to discover new ways of aiding the growing settlement population. The behavior of the squatters themselves has also shaped policy, most recently and most dramatically in the patterns of invasions that occurred during the Velasco period. The game of squatters and oligarchs has thus been played from both sides, and the perceived impact of settlement policy in each period and the reaction of the squatters to settlement policy has itself been a factor in influencing subsequent policy change.

Limitation of Pluralism and
Subtypes of Authoritarian Rule

Among the many aspects of policy change that have occurred in this context of modernization and changing political coalitions, the most important from the point of view of this analysis concerns the evolving approaches to the limitation of political pluralism—the evolving approaches to the use of state resources to inhibit the emergence of autonomous political groups and to control or channel their political demand making. These alternative approaches are of particular interest because they may be used as a starting point for distinguishing among subtypes of authoritarian rule.

Four different approaches to limiting pluralism emerged in the present analysis: the use of paternalism to encourage dependency; the encouragement of self-help and autonomy which is intended to limit political demand making and atomize the settlement population politically; direct repression; and comprehensive control based on carefully articulated hierarchical structures which link the settlements to the state. Three of the policy periods considered here have involved various combinations of these approaches to limiting pluralism. In the remaining period, the period of party politics, a clear design for elite-mass relations was reflected in settlement policy but the limitation of pluralism was not a central element in this design (see Table 5).

Under Odría, settlement policy encouraged a paternalistic, dependent, informal, clientelistic relationship between the state and the settlement residents which was oriented around charity. This constituted a technique for limiting pluralism because it was part of the campaign against Apra and

TABLE 5. Evolving Economic and Political Interests
and Methods of Limiting Pluralism

Policy Period	Economic and Political Interests around which Settlement Policy is Oriented	Method of Limiting Pluralism: Desired Linkage between Settlement Resident and the State
Odría (1948–56)	Settlement policy shaped by needs of anti-Apra coalition of export elite and military to develop alternative mode of elite mass relations; role of traditional haciendas as a "model"	Paternalistic; dependent; informal; oriented toward charity; clientelistic
Prado-Beltrán (1956–60)	Settlement policy shaped by economic interests of export oligarchy and associated elements of the urban commercial elite	Autonomous; government aid serves to encourage self-help
Period of Party Politics (1961–68)	Settlement policy shaped by political interest of parties in gaining electoral support	Absence of a well-defined strategy for limiting pluralism; substantial role of the state; formal policy commitments; objective criterion for who gets aid
Velasco (1968–75)	Settlement policy shaped by political interests of a new type of military reformer (produced by stalemate among the above groups) concerned with internal security and with scaling down policy commitments	Autonomous, in the sense of oriented toward self-help; but also comprehensive political control; politically incorporated, with political space filled; corporative ordering of vertical linkages

was, along with the overt repression of Apra, intended to promote an alternative pattern of linkages between the urban poor and the state that was not based on mass mobilization.

In the liberal period, settlement policy was oriented toward encouraging autonomy and self-help on the part of the poor and reducing their dependence on the state. The purpose was to limit pluralism by creating a world of self-help and homeownership for the poor in which they would learn to solve their own problems, would be less inclined to make demands on the state, and would be insulated from radical political appeals.

Following the sweeping policy commitments of the period of party politics, the period after 1968 saw a return to the concern with self-help and with encouraging autonomy from the state which characterized the earlier liberal period. At the same time, there has been an attempt to establish an elaborate hierarchical structure of political control that has no precedent in earlier periods.

For all of these periods, it should be emphasized that the present discussion is concerned with the *approach* to limiting pluralism that emerged under each government; with the *desired* linkage between the settlement resident and the state. It is obvious that there has been substantial variation in the degree to which the government has been successful in carrying out its plans for linking the settlement residents to the state. The central concern here is not with the degree to which it succeeded, but rather with the way in which it attempted to do it. It is clear, however, that the degree of success of earlier policies and the *perceptions* of the causes of earlier policy failure did influence the approach to limiting pluralism that was adopted in each successive period.

These evolving approaches to the limitation of pluralism, and hence to authoritarian rule, involve policy toward only one sector of society—a major sector of the urban poor of Lima. However, the evidence presented in the preceding chapters suggests that this particular area of policy did not vary in isolation, but rather corresponded to the overall policy adopted in each period toward the lower classes in general. Payne's broad characterization of Odría as paternalistic and the description of the role played by Odría's wife suggest that the type of relationship that Odría sought to promote between the state and the settlements was in fact more broadly characteristic of his regime. Beltrán's program, built around homeownership and self-sufficiency, was not intended only for urban squatters, but rather for the entire low-income population of Peru in both urban and rural areas. In the Velasco period, the active encouragement of semiautonomous local units that are linked to the state through a carefully controlled organizational hierarchy occurred not only in the settlements, but rather in a broad range of sectors of Peruvian society. Finally, the period of party politics—which did not appear to involve a deliberate strategy for limiting pluralism—was likewise a period of freer political competition and higher levels of political mobilization in other sectors of Peruvian society— particularly peasant mobilization. Hence, though settlement policy involves only a small "sample" of the total universe of public policies which define the type of political rule present in each period, it appears that for the periods considered here, settlement policy has reflected to a substantial degree the overall pattern of rule with respect to the lower classes.

Political Control and Autonomy
of the Political Sphere

The findings of this study also permit certain observations regarding two hypotheses that were discussed in the first chapter concerning the relationship between modernization and the degree of coerciveness and comprehensiveness of political control and the degree of autonomy of the political sphere. With regard to political control, the most recent, and in a sense the most "advanced," period appears to involve the most comprehensive political control. However, there is not a clear trend in this direction. The next most coercive period is that of Odría, with its extensive repression of Apra. The other two periods were less coercive. The conclusion one reaches regarding the link between modernization and coercion thus depends on how much weight one places on the high degree of control in the final period as opposed to the fluctuation in the intermediate periods. An appropriate conclusion might be that though higher levels of modernization may bring sharp increases in the coerciveness and comprehensiveness of political control, this trend may be subject to reversal or modification in subsequent periods.

With regard to the autonomy of the political sphere with respect to class interests, there appears to be a more decisive trend. The first two periods were ones in which class interests played a central role in shaping settlement policy. Odría's coup was in considerable measure sponsored by the export elite, and though the policies of his government did subsequently diverge sharply from the interests of that group, his approach to the settlements clearly reflected a goal that he shared with this economic sector, that of undermining Apra. There were also some links—though far more indirect—between the elite of the traditional haciendas of the highlands and Odría's policies. It was argued that the pattern of elite-mass relations characteristic of this sector may have served as a model for Odría's approach to the settlements and that his settlement policy encouraged a pattern of urbanization that was congruent with the interests of this traditional sector. The second period of settlement policy involved an even more direct application of the interests and ideology of an economic sector—the export elite and associated urban commercial interests—to settlement policy.

In the third and fourth periods, there has been a more central role of interests that may be called political rather than economic. The style of policy in the period of party politics was attributed to the distinctive needs of parties as a particular type of *political* organization. This finding regarding the role of parties would appear to involve the issue of reaching a high enough level of modernization to make it possible to sustain moderately well institutionalized parties that develop their own maintenance needs as organizations. However, two points of caution are in order regarding this finding. First, several earlier periods in Peruvian history—most importantly the period from 1945 to 1948—involved a major role of at least one party, though not the degree of sustained multiparty competition of the late Prado and Belaúnde periods. Second, a major purpose of the Velasco government was to eliminate the form of party politics and party competition that existed in the years prior to Velasco's coup. Hence, the tendency toward a greater role of highly institutionalized political parties should not be overstated.

The findings regarding the differentiation of the political sphere in the fourth period are considerably more clear-cut. In this period, the particular needs of the military, as part of the state itself, to protect itself as an organization have clearly played a central role in shaping all areas of policy, including settlement policy, in a way that has no precedent in earlier periods. Though the concern of the military to protect itself as an institution within the Peruvian state played some role in Ordría's coup in 1948, there is a sharp contrast in the degree to which this concern led the military to act in a cohesive way as an institution. Once Odría's coup had occurred, he proceeded to rule in a relatively personalistic fashion to such an extent that the 1948 to 1956 period could hardly be characterized as one of a "military government." The Velasco period, by contrast, was one of the most important examples in Latin American history of political rule by the military as an institution. The finding regarding the changing role of the military would seem to represent an instance of the tendency toward a greater degree of autonomy of the state—or elements of the state—from economic interests noted in the first chapter.

Further Comparative Perspectives

Though the primary focus of this research has been on the analysis of change over time within a single national context, the introduction of selected comparisons with other countries represents a useful supplementary source of insights about settlement policy.

Relation of Settlements to the National Political System

The distinct patterns of linkage between the squatter settlements and the state which emerged in the four periods of policy considered in this study show clearly that there is no inevitable relationship between squatter settlements and the national political system. Neither the threatening image of settlements evoked at the beginning of the first chapter nor the reality of manipulation of the settlements which has been an important theme of this book is inevitable. Rather, the political consequences of the existence of settlements depend on the political context.[2] During the period considered in this study, that context has changed greatly and the linkages between the settlements and the political system have changed accordingly.

This finding concerning the importance of the political context is supported by comparisons with other countries, where differences in the political context have produced both greater radicalism in settlements than is found in Peru and cases of even greater powerlessness of settlement residents in relation to the state. Settlements played an important part in the mobilization of the political left in Chile prior to the election of Allende, and support of invasions by leftist parties was a central feature of this mobilization.[3] Though there has been some involvement of the political left in settlements in Peru, and though there is some evidence of a similar limited role in Mexico,[4] the Chilean case appears to be unique in Latin America. This uniqueness is obviously explained by the fact that, until September 1973, Chile had the most powerful and autonomous political left of any country in Latin America, except Cuba.

In other countries, the extensive eradication of settlements suggests that they are even more powerless in their relations with the government than in Peru, where eradication has been an occasional, but not a central, feature of policy. Instances of systematic policies of eradication may be found in certain periods in Brazil, Venezuela, and Argentina, and eradication is also an important feature of policy in Asian and African countries.[5] In the Central African Republic and the Ivory Coast, antisquatter policy has been taken to the remarkable extreme of literally loading cityward migrants into trucks and taking them back to the countryside.[6]

Two factors that help to explain these differences among countries are the degree of lower-class political mobilization and the coercive capacity of the state. In Brazil, Argentina, and Venezuela, in the context of moderate to high degrees of lower-class mobilization, it is only because of the relatively great coercive capacity of the state that eradication is possible. In Brazil and Argentina, this was the degree of coercion associated with the "bureaucratic-authoritarian" phase of authoritarian rule.[7] In Africa, in the context of relatively weak states, it is only because of the low degree of lower-class political mobilization that eradication has been possible. In Peru, the relatively high—though episodic—degree of lower-class mobilization combined with an only moderate coercive capacity of the state has made these more harsh policies toward settlements less likely.

These comparisons help to place in perspective the range of variation represented in the changes in settlement policy that have been considered in this study. Though these changes have been substantial, certain policy alternatives, and certain alternative forms of settlement politics, have not been serious possibilities in Peru. Extensive eradication, though occasionally discussed, was never very likely, and radicalism in the settlements has at times been feared, but has never appeared to be imminent. In terms of this broader comparison, certain important features of the experience of settlements have thus been relatively unchanging in Peru.

Policy Change in Authoritarian and Democratic Settings

An implicit comparison that has guided this study involves the idea that policy change in authoritarian settings has certain distinctive characteristics. This distinction between authoritarian and democratic developmental patterns is not intended as a sharp dichotomy, with totally distinct processes of change occurring within each of the patterns. During the period considered in this study, Peru went through a phase that was clearly more democratic. Similarly, the relationship between political crises and changing patterns of political control, an important feature of authoritarian systems, is unquestionably present in democratic countries as well, as a well-known study of "regulating the poor" in the United States has demonstrated.[8] The difference between authoritarian and democratic systems is rather one in which certain patterns or tendencies are more accentuated in one type of system than in the other.

This combination of similarities and differences emerges clearly in the parallels and contrasts between the successive conceptions of elite-mass relations which have been reflected in settlement policy in Peru and in the major stages of welfare policy in certain countries of Northwestern Europe which are also among the most important countries to have followed a democratic developmental path. It has been suggested that there are three principal stages of social welfare policy in these countries.[9] During the period of nation building and mercantilism—roughly through the end of the eighteenth century—a paternalistic approach based on the ideas of "dependence and protection" prevailed.[10] During the period of industrialization and liberalism, which corresponded roughly to the nineteenth century, a laissez-faire approach predominated under which the poor were responsible for taking care of themselves.[11] The poor were to be taught self-reliance, and the one kind of charity that could be permitted was that which helped the poor to help themselves.[12] The third phase involves the gradual growth of the modern welfare state, based on broad programs of state assistance providing benefits on terms that are highly formalized in law and are not based on a personalistic or charitable conception of the relation of the state to the poor.

There is a striking similarity between the general features, and many of the details, of the conception of the appropriate form of elite-mass relations that characterized each of these three stages in the history of welfare policy in these democratic countries and the first three periods of settlement policy in Peru. At the same time, however, there are also major differences. For present purposes, perhaps the most significant difference involves the time span over which the successive conceptions of elite-mass relations have evolved. Transitions that took place over decades or even hundreds of years in certain advanced countries have occurred in settlement policy in Peru within a period of just a few years. This collapsing or telescoping of stages in the evolution of public policy is obviously analogous to, and is in part a consequence of, the tendency in Latin America toward an often incongruous juxtaposition of traditional and modern political groups that led to the characterization of Latin American politics as a "living museum."[13]

Granted that these differences between the European and the Peruvian experience exist, it is relevant to ask whether they have, in fact, made any difference. It appears that they have, and that they help to account both for the extent to which the policies that have been pursued have accomplished their intended purposes and for the emergence of a fourth phase of policy in Peru which does not have a counterpart in the evolution of welfare policy in these European countries. The question of whether the policies have accomplished their intended purposes is particularly interesting with reference to the period of party politics. In the advanced countries of Europe, social welfare legislation was, broadly speaking, successful. In Peru, by contrast, Law 13517 committed the government to programs that it failed to carry out, thereby contributing to the atmosphere of crisis and instability of the late 1960s. Whereas in one setting formal, sweeping policy commitments helped to meet the problems of the day and enhanced the legitimacy of the state,[14] in Peru they aggravated the problems of the day and pushed the nation to a new authoritarian stage that has no counterpart in these advanced countries.

The causes of this policy failure are obviously complex, and one would not wish to make an overly simplified argument that Peru was not "ready" to apply a law such as 13517. Nonetheless, it was in part because of the problems posed by the "political museum" of diverse groups and the telescoping of stages and the simultaneous confrontation of a wide variety of developmental tasks that policy failure was so widespread under Belaúnde. During this period, Peru was faced simultaneously with the problems of liquidating the inequalities and injustices associated with the traditional haciendas of the highlands and of dealing with the land seizures through which peasants sought to end these inequalities; reconciling the power and policy preferences of the export elite with the desire to alter Peru's relation with foreign investors, encourage domestic industry, and develop a stronger state; and meeting the demands for mass welfare at a time when Peru was still a relatively poor and undeveloped country with a weak state and an inefficient bureaucracy. This telescoping of stages is obviously not the only explanation for why Peru is following an authoritarian developmental path. It does, however, appear to be an important part of the explanation for why Peru's authoritarian tendency crystallized in the way it did in the final phase of settlement policy.

Conclusion: The Timing of Political Change

These findings regarding contrasts in developmental experiences may be used as the basis for some concluding observations about the timing of political change and policy change in Peru.

The spread of economic and social modernization to the Third World occurs in substantial measure through powerful forces of diffusion, involving both free imitation on the part of later modernizing countries or subunits within them and imposition from the advanced centers of modernity.[15] Both similarities and differences in developmental patterns can be understood in terms of diffusion. Because of the importance of international diffusion, it is hardly surprising that the sequence of ideologies of welfare and of approaches to structuring the relationship between the state and the poor which have appeared in North Atlantic countries should emerge in a somewhat similar form in a later developing country such as Peru. At the same time, the presence of diffusion makes it possible for Peru to move through this sequence in a relatively short period of time. Because all of these phases had emerged in Europe well before the first period of settlement policy considered here, all of them were available to Peru as models in a way that facilitated the telescoping of stages noted above.[16]

This pattern is not only characteristic of settlement policy in Peru, but also corresponds to the broader finding that major phases in the evolution of the role of the state in society, which were in some degree separated into well-defined periods in the most advanced countries of Europe, often appear simultaneously or in close succession in the Third World.[17] The adoption of new policies may therefore often occur at a point when the state's capabilities for policy performance are far more limited, producing a type of policy failure that is less likely in the countries where these approaches were first invented.[18]

Within Latin America, this phenomenon of "premature" political change appears to be particularly important in Peru, as was suggested in Chapter I in the analysis of the emergence of Apra. It was argued that within the framework of comparison among Latin American countries, the pattern of enclave modernization followed by Peru produced at an exceptionally low level of modernization an innovative, unusually well institutionalized political party that over many decades has had a decisive impact both on the types of national political regimes that have appeared in Peru and on settlement policy. Hence, while many Latin American countries have been exposed to the dilemmas that arise from the collapsing of developmental stages and from the political stalemates that often occur when highly disparate combinations of traditional and modern political groups are juxtaposed within the same political system, these tendencies have been especially pronounced in Peru.

The argument is obviously not that the developmental pattern followed by earlier modernizers was "natural" or "correct" and that the Peruvian pattern should be viewed as a distortion of available models of modernization. Rather, because of international diffusion, modernization occurs in different ways in different historical settings, creating distinctive opportunities and dilemmas in each setting. The Peruvian experience differs both from that of the earliest modernizers of Europe and also from that of earlier modernizers within Latin America, just as important differences exist between earlier and later modernizers within Europe. The contrasting experience of many different contexts of modernization must be considered if one is to gain an adequate perspective on the variegated relationships that have emerged between economic and social modernization and political change.

Appendix I

Sources of Data

In conducting research on Lima squatter settlements, I was fortunate to be able to rely on a rich body of earlier literature on the settlements. On the Peruvian side, research carried out in the middle to late 1950s by José Matos Mar, the Comisión para la Reforma Agraria y la Vivienda, and the Fondo Nacional de Salud y Bienestar Social provided the first reliable information on the social and economic characteristics of settlements. More recent work had been completed by the Centro de Investigaciones Sociales por Muestreo of the Peruvian Ministry of Labor and a number of studies by Peruvians were just being completed at the time of my work in Lima. Foreign researchers had likewise contributed greatly to the understanding of the settlements. The work of Turner and Mangin had extended earlier insights regarding opportunities for self-help and community development in the settlements and had focused international attention on the positive role that settlements can play in urban development. Subsequent research by Goldrich, Dietz, Powell, Manaster, and others had added important insights regarding the political characteristics of the settlements.

This literature was limited, however, in its analysis of the differing types of settlement formation and of the evolution of government policy toward settlements. Some useful descriptions of invasions and other types of settlement formation were presented, but there was not sufficient data on a large number of cases of formation to permit an adequate assessment of the relative importance of each type. Previous research also lacked historical depth. It generally focused on settlement politics in the later 1950s or the 1960s and therefore did not take into account the very different patterns of settlement development of the later 1940s and early 1950s.

The present research sought to remedy this lack of data on settlement formation and the lack of historical perspective through the collection of extensive new data on the formation of settlements in Lima. This was done primarily through interviews with present and former settlement leaders who had been involved in the formation of their settlements and who were familiar with the history of the formation. These interviews were organized around a questionnaire prepared by the author using closed and open-ended questions to discover in the greatest possible detail how the settlement was formed. The interviews provided detailed information on the role of the government in settlement formation and hence permitted the reconstruction of an important aspect of the history of government policy toward settlements.

The questions covered a series of issues such as how the group that founded the settlement was originally organized; their reasons for moving to a settlement; how they selected a site; outside aid they may have had in preparing the occupation; who owned the land; how they occupied the site; how many people occupied the site; the reaction of the owner and the police; negotiations with public authorities over police intervention and eviction; the speed with which the settlement grew; and related questions. The questionnaire was designed in such a way that if the respondent had information about an earlier attempt to occupy the site, the entire set of questions could be repeated to collect information on this earlier attempt. Questions regarding the respondent's perceptions of how the community was developing were also included.

Respondents were generally cooperative and were pleased to be asked about what they usually viewed as an exciting and heroic period of their lives. Since in many cases they were no longer important community leaders, they were particularly glad to have an opportunity to discuss the earlier history of the settlement in which they had an important role.

A number of means were employed to check the quality of the information on the formation itself. The questionnaire, which was applied in 72 different settlements, was reapplied in the cases in which the information in the first interview seemed unreliable or in which the history of the formation was of particularly great interest. Additional information was collected from published sources, newspaper archives, archives in government housing offices, and interviews with government administrators who had long experience with settlements.[1] Aside from assuring greater accuracy in the tabulations of types of invasions, this information served to provide confirmation from at least two or three sources of virtually all of the most important or dramatic cases of settlement formation. Since different versions of what happened were sometimes offered by people who had different interests to promote or protect, this cross-checking was important. These additional data also provided detailed information on a number of cases that were not included in the survey of settlement leaders, particularly cases of formation after 1968. It also provided less complete information on a large number of other cases.

The Sample

The selection of communities for the application of the questionnaire was deliberately biased toward two types of settlements—those for which it was suspected that there had been some political support for the formation and larger settlements. Cases of suspected political involvement were emphasized because, in addition to estimating the proportion of settlements that were formed with political support, it was also a purpose of the research to develop as clear a picture as possible of what this support consists of when it occurs. This bias is obviously taken into account in any attempt to infer characteristics of the universe from the sample. The sample also overrepresented large settlements, whose size ranges up to 20,000 or 30,000 residents and in one case exceeds 100,000. These are obviously more important in terms of their contribution to solving the Lima housing shortage than the small settlements, which may contain only 100 or 200 residents.

The following procedure was used in choosing settlements for the application of the questionnaire: (1) Thirty-five settlements were selected because they were represented in the sample of the CISM survey discussed in Chapter II. This survey used a carefully drawn, multistage, clustered probability sample in which all settlement residents initially had an equal chance of being interviewed. Hence, the probability that any one settlement was represented in the sample was exactly proportional to its size. Because of this, all of the larger settlements are represented among the 35. Using the sample of this CISM survey thus provided a convenient criterion for selecting communities that assured adequate representation of the larger, and hence more important, settlements. The overlap in the samples also permitted the simultaneous analysis of the data from the two sources. (2) Many additional settlements were selected because they had histories that were suspected to be of particular interest, especially in cases where other sources of information suggested that there had been some political support for the formation. (3) Still other cases were chosen because of proximity to settlements chosen by the first and second criteria.

The data analysis is based on two samples: A smaller sample of 84 settlements on which detailed information was available and a larger sample that includes an additional 52 settlements on which less detailed information was collected. The data on the additional 52 cases in which the questionnaire was not applied came from the files of the Oficina de Barrios Marginales of the Junta Nacional de la Vivienda and from data compiled by Plan Metropolitana de Lima. Because of the emphasis in the application of the questionnaire on including larger settlements, the smaller sample includes 81.7 percent of the total settlement population of Lima, even though it only includes 40.4 percent of the settlements. The larger sample includes 90.2 percent of the residents and 65.4 percent of the settlements. These estimates of the size of the sample and universe cover the period through 1972.

It should be noted that 2 settlements that no longer exist are included in the smaller sample, as well as several cases of unsuccessful attempts to form settlements. At certain points in the analysis, 12 additional cases of unsuccessful attempts to occupy land on which a settlement was later formed are included in the tabulations. It was decided not to include these 12 in the smaller sample or in the definition of the universe, since that would have involved counting the same land twice. In the cases of unsuccessful formation in the smaller sample, on the other hand, the land was never successfully occupied, so that including them in the definition of the universe does not involve counting the same land twice.

The Universe

There are various ways in which the universe from which these cases come may be defined, but a reasonable one—excluding all known cases of formation by illegal renting or purchase (see below)—consists of 208 settlements, with a total population of 841,075 in 1972. The estimate of the universe was derived from the results of a 1970 census of Lima settlements which reported the existence of 273 settlements with a population of 761,755.[2] Several modifications had to be made of these figures. First, there were 10 cases of settlement formation or attempted formation between 1970 and 1972. Second, 23 older communities were added which are considered settlements for the purposes of this research but have been excluded from government lists. This included the 2 cases of settlements that no longer exist. Third, 45 communities formed through illegal renting and purchase were excluded. These had been recognized as settlements under Peruvian squatter settlement legislation, but were formed through the illegal renting or sale of land to low-income families who built houses on the land. These areas tended to be subdivided and sublet, following a pattern of development quite different from a squatter settlement. Hence they were not included in the analysis. Because these communities are relatively small, the decision to exclude them has little effect on the definition of the universe in terms of population. As was indicated above, the 12 cases of unsuccessful invasions on land that was subsequently occupied were not counted in the definition of the universe.

This leaves a total of 261 settlements. An additional problem with this figure is that it includes a number of small communities that had been studied by a government housing office in a survey carried out in 1961 and declared not to be settlements on the basis of criteria that corresponded closely to those used on this research. It is impossible to estimate the exact proportion, but an estimate was made on the following basis. In addition to the 136 settlements in the larger sample, it was possible to determine that 21 more communities were settlements, even though no detailed historical data were available for them, giving a total of 156 known settlements. Of the remaining 105 settlements—the difference between 156 and 261—we may make what is probably a conservative assumption that half were communities that had been excluded in the 1961 survey and therefore should not be considered settlements. This would leave a total of 208 settlements with a population of 841,075. The estimate of half is obviously a very rough guess, but even if the correct proportion that should be excluded is considerably smaller, it makes little difference in terms of the population of the communities involved, since all of the settlements about which there is uncertainty are very small.

As was indicated above, the sample does include 2 settlements that no longer exist, as well as some cases of unsuccessful attempts to form settlements. There may, of course, be other cases of settlements that no longer exist, and there are certainly other cases of unsuccessful invasions. Ideally, these should be included in the definition of the universe, but since no information is available on them, this is obviously not possible.

Other Interview Data

Apart from analyzing the role of the Peruvian government in the formation of settlements, this research also seeks to characterize other aspects of settlement policy. This part of the analysis relies on documents from government housing offices, published analyses of housing and settlement policy, newspaper reports, and extensive interviewing among present and former housing officials, architects who were interested in settlement policy, former congressmen, and settlement residents. In cases in which an important interpretation relies on an interview source, the type of source involved, but not the identity of the source, is indicated. Though a large portion of this interviewing was carried out in 1968–69, supplementary visits were made to Lima in August to September of 1972 and in August of 1974.

Appendix II

Tables

TABLE II.1. Selected Data on the Growth of Lima

	1	2	3	4	5	6
	Lima Population (Metropolitan Area)	Lima Settlement Population (Metropolitan Area)	Settlement Population/ Metropolitan Population	Lima Population/ National Population	Lima Presidential Vote (Department of Lima)	Lima Vote/ National Vote
1908	154,615	–	–	3.9%	–	–
1919	199,200	–	–	4.2%	19,810	9.7%
1931	341,720	–	–	6.2%	34,747	28.2%
1940	520,528	Probably less than 5,000	Less than 1.0%	8.4%	–	–
1961	1,578,298	318,262	20.2%	17.0%	757,403 (1963)	41.7% (1963)
1972	3,317,000	841,075	25.4%	24.2%	–	–

Sources: The data in columns 1, 4, 5, and 6 were adapted from tables generously supplied by Carl Herbold. The sources for columns 1 and 4 are Dirección de Salubridad Pública, *Censo de la Provincia de Lima de 1908* (Lima: 1915); Dirección de Estadística, *Resumenes del Censo de las Provincias de Lima y Callao de 1920* (Lima: 1927); Junta Departamental Pro-desocupados, *Censo de las provincias de Lima y Callo en 1931* (Lima: 1931) p. 46; Dirección Nacional de Estadística, *Censo Nacional de Población y Ocupación de 1940*, Vol. 5, p. 5; A. Arca Parró, "La ciudad capital de la República y el Censo Nacional de 1940", *Estadística Peruana* 1, No. 1 (1945), pp. 24-29; and Dirección Nacional de Estadística y Censos, *Centros Poblados*, Vol. 3. The figure for 1972 is a preliminary estimate of the results of the 1972 census released by the Oficina Nacional de Estadística y Censos as reported in *La Prensa*, 23 September 1972, p. 1. The national population figure for 1908 is from Arthur S. Banks, *Cross-Polity Time-Series Data*. Interpolations were carried out by Carl Herbold in a few cases to provide data for comparable years.

The election data are from *Dario de Debates de la Asamblea Nacional*, Vol. 1, pp. 166-70; *Extracto Estadístico del Perú: 1931-1932-1933*, pp. 265-66; Basadre, *Historia de la República del Perú*, Vol. 14, p. 168; Rudolph Gómez, *The Peruvian Administrative System*, p. 27; Richard W. Patch, "The Peruvian Elections of 1963," p. 498-513 in Robert D. Tomasek, ed., *Latin American Politics*, p. 509; and Carlos A. Astiz, *Pressure Groups and Power Elites in Peruvian Politics*, p. 50.

The estimate of the settlement population in 1940 is based on data compiled by the author. The figure for 1961 is from the national census of that year, cited above. The derivation of the figure for 1972 is described in Appendix I. As is indicated in the Postscript to Chapter VII, the population has increased substantially since 1972.

TABLE II.2. Police Reaction[a]
(Government Authorizations and Invasions from Smaller
Sample, Plus 12 Prior Invasions)

Police Reaction	Number of Settlements	Percent
Did not appear	32	38.1
Came but did nothing	6	7.1
Only prevented arrival of additional families	7	8.3
Symbolic eviction effort only	8	9.5
Serious attempt to evict, but failed	8	9.5
Successful eviction	22	26.2
Incomplete data	1	1.2
TOTAL	84	99.9

[a]In this and the following tables, the data cover the period through 1972.

TABLE II.3. Types of Land Ownership
(Government Authorizations and Invasions from Smaller
Sample, Plus 12 Prior Invasions)

Ownership	Smaller Sample	Percent	Prior Invasions	Percent	Total
Public	37	51.4	1	8.3	38
In dispute	20	27.8	9	75.0	29
Private	14	19.4	2	16.7	16
Incomplete data	1	1.4	–	–	1
TOTAL	72	100.0	12	100.0	84

TABLE II.4. Police Reaction by Ownership of Land
(Government Authorizations and Invasions from Smaller
Sample, Plus 12 Prior Invasions)

Police Reaction	Public	In Dispute	Private	Incomplete Data	Total
Did not appear	24	6	2	–	32
Came but did nothing	3	3	–	–	6
Only prevented arrival of additional families	3	4	–	–	7
Symbolic eviction effort only	5	2	1	–	8
Serious attempt to evict but failed	1	4	3	–	8
Successful eviction	2	10	10	–	22
Incomplete data	–	–	–	1	1
TOTAL	38	29	16	1	84

TABLE II.5. Police Reaction by Type of Formation
(Government Authorizations and Invasions from Smaller
Sample, Plus 12 Prior Invasions)

Police Reaction	Government Authorization	Invasion	Total
Did not appear	26	6	32
Came but did nothing	2	4	6
Only prevented arrival of additional families	3	4	7
Symbolic eviction effort only	2	6	8
Serious attempt to evict, but failed	1	7	8
Successful eviction	—	22	22
Incomplete data	1	—	1
TOTAL	35	49	84

TABLE II.6. Role of Political Groups by Police Reaction
(Government Authorizations and Invasions from Smaller
Sample, Plus 12 Prior Invasions)

POLICE REACTION	Informal government intervention prior to occupation of land	Public authorization prior to occupation of land	Informal government intervention, after occupation of land	Intervention by nonpresidential party	Possible government involvement but ambiguous or insufficient information	No apparent political involvement	Total
Did not appear	9	15	–	2	3	3	32
Came but did nothing	2	–	2	–	2	–	6
Only prevented arrival of additional families	1	1	2	1	–	2	7
Symbolic eviction effort only	2	–	1	1	3	1	8
Serious attempt to evict, but failed	1	–	5	–	2	–	8
Successful eviction	–	–	–	1	4	17	22
Incomplete data	–	–	–	1	–	–	1
TOTAL	15	16	10	6	14	23	84

TABLE II.7. Landownership by Type of Formation
(Government Authorizations and Invasions from Smaller
Sample, Plus 12 Prior Invasions)

TYPE OF FORMATION

OWNERSHIP	Government Authorization	Percent	Invasion, Main Occupation	Percent	Prior Invasion	Percent	Total
Public	26	74.3	11	29.7	1	8.3	38
In dispute	6	17.1	14	37.8	9	75.0	29
Private	2	5.7	12	32.4	2	16.7	16
Incomplete data	1	2.9	–	–	–	–	1
TOTAL	35	100.0	37	99.9	12	100.0	84

TABLE II.8. Role of Private and Public Urban
Development and Real Estate Interests
in Settlement Formation
(Smaller Sample)[a]

Immediate Interest Served	Number of Settlements	Percent
To aid eviction for a public or private development project	17	28
Eviction by suspicious fire	2	3
Eviction from two or more slum areas	3	5
Rural eviction	3	5
Would-be private owner to establish claim to land	1	2
Would-be public owner to establish claim to land	1	2
No evidence of involvement by urban development or real estate interests	33	55
TOTAL	60	100

[a]Includes only cases for which appropriate information was available.

TABLE II.9. Type of Formation by President
(Larger Sample)

| PRESIDENT | TYPE OF FORMATION | | | | |
	Government Authorization	Invasion	Gradual Occupation	Other	Total
Pre-Sánchez Cerro (1900–30)	–	1	1	–	2
Sánchez Cerro (1930–31, 1931–33)	1	1	1	–	3
Benavides (1933–39)	1	3	4	–	8
Prado (1939–45)	–	–	6	2	8
1945–ambiguous	–	–	5	–	5
Bustamante (1945–48)	1	6	8	1	16
Odría (1948–56)	11	11	8	–	30
1956–ambiguous	–	2	–	–	2
Prado (1956–62)	11	11	7	1	30
1962–ambiguous	–	1	1	–	2
Pérez Godoy (1962–63)	–	2	–	–	2
Lindley (1963)	1	2	–	–	3
Belaúnde (1963–68)	12	3	–	–	15
Velasco (1968–72 only)	3	7	–	–	10
TOTAL	41	50	41	4	136

TABLE II.10. Role of Political Groups by President
(Government Authorizations and Invasions from
Smaller Sample)

PRESIDENT	Informal government intervention prior to occupation of land	Public authorization prior to occupation of land	Informal government intervention, after occupation of land	Intervention by nonpresidential party	Possible government involvement but ambiguous or insufficient information	No apparent political involvement	Total
Sánchez Cerro	1	–	–	–	1	–	2
Benavides	1	–	–	–	–	–	1
Prado–I	–	–	–	–	–	–	0
Bustamante	–	–	5	–	–	1	6
Odría	6	4	2	1	2	3	18
Prado–II	5	2	3	1	2	3	16
Pérez Goduy	–	–	–	–	1	–	1
Lindley	–	1	–	2	–	–	3
Belaúnde	2	6	–	5	1	1	15
Velasco	–	3	–	–	–	7	10
TOTAL	15	16	10	9	7	15	72

Notes*

Chapter I

1. In using the expression *oligarchic*, I intend to refer to the fact that the principal agricultural elites in Peru, commonly referred to as "the oligarchy" by Peruvians, have until recently held substantial power. I do not mean to imply that they are all-powerful or to take sides in the debate as to whether an oligarchy really "exists" in Peru. For a sample of this debate, see Instituto de Estudios Peruanos, *La Oligarquía en el Perú*. For an excellent discussion of criteria for identifying an oligarchy, see James L. Payne, "The Oligarchy Muddle." The agreement of authors such as Bourricaud and Larson and Bergman concerning the major political role of the oligarchy in Peru obviously does not apply to the period after 1968. See François Bourricaud, *Power and Society in Contemporary Peru*, p. 14, and Magali Sarfatti Larson and Arlene Eisen Bergman, *Social Stratification in Peru*, p. 257. A discussion of the authoritarian traits of the Peruvian political system is presented below.

2. See José Matos Mar, "Migration and Urbanization—The 'Barriadas' of Lima"; Daniel Goldrich et al., "The Political Integration of Lower-Class Urban Settlements in Chile and Peru"; William Mangin, "Urbanization Case History in Peru," "Latin American Squatter Settlements: A Problem and a Solution," and "Squatter Settlements"; John F. C. Turner, "Lima Barriadas Today," "Lima's *Barriadas* and *Corralones*: Suburbs vs. Slums," "Barriers and Channels for Housing Development in Modernizing Countries," and "Uncontrolled Urban Settlement: Problems and Policies"; Sandra Powell, "Political Participation in the Barriadas: A Case Study"; Henry A. Dietz, "Urban Squatter Settlements in Peru: A Case History and Analysis"; and Frank M. Andrews and George W. Phillips, "'The Squatters of Lima: Who They Are and What They Want."

3. Gino Germani and Kalman Silvert, "Politics, Social Structure, and Military Intervention in Latin America," in Peter G. Snow, ed., *Government and Politics in Latin America* (New York: Holt, Rinehart, and Winston, 1967), pp. 299–318, represents an early and important step toward this approach. The more recent statement that most explicitly adopts this perspective is Guillermo A. O'Donnell, *Modernization and Bureaucratic-Authoritarianism: Studies in South American Politics.* Other well-known studies that are particularly relevant to this approach include Philippe C. Schmitter, *Interest Conflict and Political Change in Brazil*; Fernando Henrique Cardoso and Enzo Faletto, *Dependencia y desarrollo en América Latina*; and Cardoso, "Associated-

*For the full citation of works cited in shortened form, see the Bibliography.

153

Dependent Development: Theoretical and Practical Implications," in Alfred Stepan, ed., *Authoritarian Brazil: Origins, Policies, and Future* (New Haven: Yale University Press, 1973), pp. 142–178.

4. This thesis has been elaborated in much cross-national literature on Latin America and elsewhere, including work by Lipset, Coleman, Hagen, Cutright, Simpson, Alker, Neubauer, Olsen, and many others. A major example of a qualitative study that adopted this perspective is John J. Johnson's *Political Change in Latin America: The Emergence of the Middle Sectors.* See also Tad Szulc, *The Twilight of the Tyrants* (New York: Henry Holt, 1959).

5. Barrington Moore, Jr., *Social Origins of Dictatorship and Democracy*, especially Chapter VII.

6. This was an important assumption in much of the literature cited in note 4.

7. See the cross-national research referred to in note 4.

8. Tad Szulc, *The Twilight of the Tyrants.*

9. Alain Rouquié, "Military Revolutions and National Independence in Latin America: 1968–1971," in Philippe C. Schmitter, ed., *Military Rule in Latin America: Functions, Consequences, and Perspectives* (Beverly Hills: Sage Publications, 1973), p. 48.

10. See note 3. For useful compilations of studies of authoritarianism in Latin America, see the January 1974 issue of *The Review of Politics*, which is devoted to the closely related theme of corporatism, and James M. Malloy, ed., *Authoritarianism and Corporatism in Latin America* (Pittsburgh: University of Pittsburgh Press, forthcoming).

11. Philippe C. Schmitter, "Paths to Political Development in Latin America."

12. An example of this relationship is found in the discussion of the impact of import-substituting industrialization on the development of organized labor in Brazil, discussed in Schmitter, *Interest Politics and Political Change in Brazil*, pp. 370–71.

13. This finding frequently recurs in the literature on authoritarian politics in Latin America. See notes 3 and 10.

14. Linz's initial discussion of authoritarian regimes pointed to limited pluralism as one of four defining characteristics (see Juan J. Linz, "An Authoritarian Regime: Spain," pp. 291–341). He has recently given it an even more central place in his analysis, making the type of limitation of pluralism the basis for a typology of authoritarian regimes. See his "Notes toward a Typology of Authoritarian Regimes," pp. 25–27, and the following discussion of specific cases. Limitation of pluralism is also given a central role among the dimensions along which regimes may be arrayed in his "Totalitarian and Authoritarian Regimes."

15. The work of Cardoso, O'Donnell, and Schmitter cited above, as well as other Brazilian and North American writing on the populist and postpopulist periods in Brazil, present these arguments in considerable detail.

16. O'Donnell, *Modernization and Bureaucratic-Authoritarianism*, Chapter 1.

17. Cardoso and Faletto, *Dependencia y desarrollo en América Latina*, pp. 48 ff. and 82 ff.

18. Torcuato S. diTella, *La teoría del primer impacto del crecimiento económico.*

19. See Antonio Gramsci, *The Modern Prince and other Writings* (New York: International Publishers, 1957), pp. 174–76; Nicos Poulantzas, *Clases sociales y poder político en el estado capitalista* (Mexico City: Siglo Veintiuno Editores, 1969), pp. 169 ff.; and José Nun, *Latin America: The Hegemonic Crisis and the Military Coup.*

20. For important discussions of coalitional patterns in Latin American politics, see Charles W. Anderson, *Politics and Economic Change in Latin America: The Governing of Restless Nations*, Chapter 4, and Eldon Kenworthy, "Coalitions in the Political Development of Latin America," in Sven Groennings et al., eds., *The Study of Coalition Behavior* (New York: Holt, Rinehart and Winston, 1970).

21. This tendency is obviously one of the most dramatic features of the pattern of change that is emerging in contemporary Latin American politics, and it has been emphasized by various authors in the literature on authoritarian modernization cited above. In a broader frame of comparison, Barrington Moore, Jr., has noted the tendency for regimes following an authoritarian developmental path (which he characterizes as

"modernization through revolution from above") to go through an authoritarian, semi-parliamentary stage that evolves into facism in the face of economic and political crises (*Social Origins of Dictatorship and Democracy*, especially Chapter 8). His analysis thus points to a greater limitation of pluralism in the course of modernization. A. F. K. Organski's analysis of "syncratic" regimes points to a similar developmental trend, though he places greater emphasis on the possibilities for a return to a democratic pattern (*The Stages of Political Development*, Chapter 5).

22. See O'Donnell, "Estado y corporativismo en América Latina."

23. The growing importance in Latin America of political rule by the military *as an institution* within the state—as opposed to more personalistic rule by an individual general or group of generals—is one of the most dramatic contemporary manifestations of this trend.

24. Karl Marx, *The Eighteenth Brumaire of Louis Bonaparte*, especially pp. 120 ff. For a discussion of the place of this argument in writing on authoritarian politics, see Schmitter, "Paths to Political Development," pp. 90–92.

25. For an important statement regarding the need for caution in discussing the autonomy of the state, particularly with reference to differences in degrees of autonomy vis-à-vis different class groups, see Guillermo A. O'Donnell, "Estado y corporativismo en América Latina."

26. These periods of military rule are discussed in detail in the coming chapters and in the sources cited in the text.

27. Julio Cotler, "The Mechanics of Internal Domination and Social Change in Peru," pp. 238–40.

28. David Chaplin, *The Peruvian Industrial Labor Force*, p. 78.

29. Julio Cotler, "Estructura social y urbanización: Algunas notas comparativas," p. 6; Peter F. Klarén, *Modernization, Dislocation, and Aprismo: Origins of the Peruvian Aprista Party, 1870–1932*; and Liisa North, "Origins and Development of the Peruvian Apra Party."

30. Torcuato S. diTella, "The Working Class in Politics," in Claudio Veliz, ed., *Latin America and the Caribbean: A Handbook* (New York: Frederick Praeger, 1968), pp. 386–87.

31 See Julio Cotler, "Traditional Haciendas and Communities in a Context of Political Mobilization in Peru"; and Carlos A. Astiz, *Pressure Groups and Power Elites in Peruvian Politics*, pp. 48 ff.

32. Giorgio Alberti, "The Breakdown of Provincial Urban Power Structure and the Rise of Peasant Movements," p. 321.

33. François Bourricaud, "Structure and Function of the Peruvian Oligarchy," p. 19.

34. *Ibid.*, pp. 19–20.

35. Thomas R. Ford, *Man and Land in Peru*, p. 145; Alberti, "The Breakdown," p. 331; and Héctor Martínez, "Las migraciones internas en el Perú," p. 6.

36. Alberti, "The Breakdown," p. 316.

37. See Samuel P. Huntington, *Political Order in Changing Societies*, p. 299; Frank T. Bachmura, "Urbanization as an Alternative to Land Reform," p. 4; Gino Germani, "Emigración del campo a la ciudad y sus causas," p. 75; and J. S. MacDonald, "Agricultural Organization, Migration, and Labor Militancy in Rural Italy," pp. 61–75.

38. Martínez, "Las migraciones," p. 316.

39. J. Oscar Alers and Richard P. Appelbaum, "La migración el Perú: Un inventario de proposiciones," p. 24.

40. *Ibid.*, p. 11.

41. Aníbal Quijano, "Urbanización y tendencias de cambio en la sociedad rural en Latinoamérica," pp. 11–12. Several points of caution must be noted in analyzing the relation between migration and pressure for rural change. First, though it would seem reasonable that out-migration would reduce the pressure for political change, the contact between migrants who have left the rural community and members of the community who have stayed behind may itself stimulate rural change. However, at the individual level, leaving, as opposed to staying and working for change, clearly represents an alternative solution,

and it seems likely that landlords would see out-migration as a useful safety valve. Secondly, since our concern here is with the growth of Lima, it should be emphasized that migrants from rural areas generally do not go directly to the capital (Alers and Appelbaum, "La migración," p. 2). According to a survey carried out in late 1965, only 6.1 percent of the migrants in Lima are from population centers of 1,000 or less. (Dirección Nacional de Estadística y Censos, *Encuesta de inmigración: Lima metropolitana*, p. 9.) The reason for this is that, in general, population movement follows a pattern of step migration in which migration from rural areas to the largest urban centers is made in stages, usually over several generations. This is not to say that Lima is not an important focus for migration. In 1961, 39.9 percent of all individuals in Peru who lived outside of the province where they were born lived in Lima, and 47 percent of the population of greater Lima were migrants. (Alers and Appelbaum, "La migración," p. 3.) The relationship between migration to Lima and migration out of rural areas must be seen in terms of a pattern in which migration from provincial towns and cities to the national capital eases the pressure for employment and housing in these smaller centers and increases the incentive for people from rural areas to move to these smaller centers. Migration to Lima thus has an important, though indirect, effect on migration from the countryside.

42. See Appendix II, Table II.1.

43. Julio Cotler, "Political Crisis and Military Populism in Peru," pp. 96–98.

44. See O'Donnell, *Modernization and Bureaucratic-Authoritarianism*, pp. 56–57.

45. Cotler, "Estructura social," pp. 2–3.

46. Anderson, *Politics and Economic Change*, p. 104.

Chapter II

1. For a discussion of the criteria employed in including squatter communities in the present study, see Appendix I.

2. These terms may be found in newspaper stories on settlements in the 1950s and 1960s. The term *barrio marginado* has been used by the left, and occasionally by Apra. The expression *aberración social* appears in the title of Pablo Berckholtz Salinas, *Barrios marginales: Aberración social* (Lima: 1963).

3. See Appendix I.

4. John F. C. Turner, "Lima Barriadas Today."

5. Richard Patch, "Life in a Callejón: A Study of Urban Disorganization"; and Hugo Gutierrez Vidalón, "Tugurio: Estudio de casos."

6. Baltazar Caravedo et al., *Estudios de psiquiatría social en el Perú*, pp. 85–93.

7. I would like to acknowledge my debt to the Survey Research Center for providing access to this and other survey data. Squatter settlements were not identified in the original code for the study, and were identified by the author with the aid of sampling maps. The original code did identify two types of slum housing: *callejones* and *corralones*. *Callejones* are low-cost apartment complexes consisting of single rooms built along narrow corridors. *Corralones* are made up of single-family dwellings which are shacks resembling the houses in a poorly developed squatter settlement. These two types of housing are discussed in Patch, "Life in a Callejón"; Turner, "Lima's *Barriadas* and *Corralones*"; and PLAN-DEMET, *Estudio de tugurios en los distritos de Jesús María y la Victoria*. The findings reported here are based on data on 123 migrant heads of households in settlements and 152 in slums. When nonmigrants were included in the sample, virtually identical results emerged for every relationship considered. For a more detailed discussion of these data, see my "Squatter Settlements and the Incorporation of Migrants into Urban Life: The Case of Lima" (Monograph Series on Migration and Development, Center for International Studies, Massachusetts Institute of Technology, 1975).

8. The validity of using this comparison as a basis for making inferences about the impact of living in a settlement obviously depends on the assumption that differences in intended spending are the result of the experience of living in a settlement or a slum. An alternative interpretation of differences between these groups could be that individuals who have a certain orientation toward the future are more likely to move to a settlement and hence that the move to the settlement is the consequence, rather than the cause, of the difference in attitudes. In their discussion of research based on static-group comparisons, Campbell and Stanley have described this as the problem of selection. See Donald T. Campbell and Julian C. Stanley, *Experimental and Quasi-Experimental Designs for Research*, p. 12. The best way to deal with this problem is, of course, to have data on the same respondents before and after the move to a settlement, but this is not available. However, certain findings that emerged from the analysis, such as the effect of introducing renting as control variable in the relationship between intended spending and residence (it greatly weakened the relationship), are harder to interpret if we assume that the difference in intended spending is a result, rather than a cause, of the move to a settlement.

9. Gamma = .46, p<.05. For an introduction to the measure of association gamma, see Linton C. Freeman, *Elementary Applied Statistics*.

10. Gamma = .38, p<.01. The other survey was the Estudio de Barrios Marginales, carried out in 1967.

11. Far more slum respondents than settlement respondents—26.4 percent as opposed to 15.4 percent—found life in Lima to be the same as or worse than life in their home province.

12. Though almost all respondents report some problems, there is a larger proportion in slums—7.2 percent—who say there are no problems, as opposed to 1.6 percent in settlements. Though the absolute size of this difference is small, in relative terms the proportion of respondents in slums who say there are no problems is four and a half times as big. The value of gamma for this relationship (.65) is significant at the .05 level.

13. For a discussion of the link between the capacity to solve problems and the ability to identify them, see Albert O. Hirschman, *Journeys toward Progress*, p. 312. More settlement residents (7.3 percent) than slum residents (1.3 percent) said the problems should be solved by the residents of the community themselves. Here again, though both percentages are small, settlement residents are nearly six times more likely to give the self-help response. The value of gamma for this relationship (.71) is significant at the .05 level.

14. Only 14.8 percent of settlement respondents, as opposed to 25.2 percent of slum respondents—about two-thirds again as many—either failed to register or failed to vote.

15. On a scale of associational and party participation, 44.8 percent of the respondents in settlements, as opposed to 28.0 in slums, fell at the medium to high level.

16. Only 6.5 percent of the respondents in settlements fell into the bottom three categories on this scale, as opposed to 15.1 in slums—nearly three times as many. This scale combined questions concerning the best means to get a job, the role of education, questions involving self-help, and the use of conciliation as opposed to strikes to settle labor disputes. For a fuller discussion of this index, see my "Squatter Settlements and the Incorporation of Migrants into Urban Life: The Case of Lima."

17. The findings of Cornelius raise some doubt about the extent to which this will occur. See Wayne A. Cornelius, "Urbanization and Political Demand Making: Political Participation Among the Migrant Poor in Latin American Cities."

18. See Carlos Delgado, "Three Proposals Regarding Accelerated Urbanization Problems in Metropolitan Areas: The Lima Case."

19. See Appendix II, Table II.1.

20. See Kingsley Davis, *World Urbanization 1950–1970*, Vol. I, pp. 149–50.

21. See Charles Abrams, *Man's Struggle for Shelter in an Urbanizing World*, p. 13.

22. Alberto Alexander, *Estudio sobre la crisis de la habitación en Lima*.

23. See, for instance, Comisión para la Reforma Agraria y la Vivienda, *Report on Housing in Peru*, pp. 13–16; Walter D. Harris, et al., *Housing in Peru*, pp. 449–58; and Instituto Nacional de Planificación, *Plan de desarrollo económico y social 1967–70: Plan sectorial de vivienda*, pp. 42 ff.

24. See Corporación Nacional de la Vivienda, *Experiencias relativas de la vivienda de interés social en el Perú.*

25. Ibid., pp. 9–48.

26. This is the author's calculation based on the report of the number of units in each of a large number of different projects reported in Corporación Nacional de la Vivienda, *Experiencias relativas.*

27. Delgado, "Three Proposals," p. 296.

28. See Comisión para la Reforma Agraria y la Vivienda, *Report on Housing*, pp. 24–25; Luis Dorich T., "Urbanization and Physical Planning in Peru," pp. 283–85; Harris et al., *Housing in Peru*, pp. 405–6 and 408; Henry A. Dietz, "Urban Squatter Settlements in Peru," p. 354; and Allan G. Austin and Sherman Lewis, *Urban Government for Metropolitan Lima*, p. 140.

29. This figure is a rough estimate for this year based on Table II.1 in Appendix II. For a detailed discussion of problems of estimating the total settlement population, see Appendix I.

30. For a general discussion of this issue, see Joan M. Nelson, "New Policies toward Squatter Settlements: Legalization versus Traditional Planners' Standards."

31. This expression was suggested in a personal communication by Vilmar Faria.

32. Charles W. Anderson, *Politics and Economic Change in Latin America*, pp. 162–83.

33. Major early statements in this tradition include Louis Wirth, "Urbanism as a Way of Life," and Robert Redfield, "The Folk Society." Schoultz has traced the origins of this tradition of research back to Tönnies, Weber, and Simmel. See Lars Schoultz, "Urbanization and Political Change in Latin America."

34. Cornelius has provided an excellent inventory of propositions involving this theme that have been presented in the work of forty-one different authors. See Wayne A. Cornelius, Jr., "The Political Sociology of City-Ward Migration in Latin America: Toward Empirical Theory," Table 1.

35. Oscar Lewis, "Urbanization without Breakdown: A Case Study."

36. Oscar Lewis, "Further Observations on the Folk-Urban Continuum and Urbanization with Special Reference to Mexico City."

37. Many of these explanations have been noted in Joan M. Nelson, *Migrants, Urban Poverty, and Instability in Developing Nations.*

38. Ibid., pp. 15–16.

39. Ibid., p. 70; and Cornelius, "The Political Sociology," pp. 115–16. Both stress the importance of considering the political context.

40. Janice Elaine Perlman, "The Fate of Migrants in Rio's Favelas: Portrait of the People" (Paper presented at a Conference on Recent Research on Rural-Urban Migration, M.I.T., 1971); and Susan Eckstein, "Theory and Methods in the Study of Poverty and the Politics of Poverty: The Substitution of a Social-Economic Structural Approach for an Individualistic Cultural Approach" (Paper presented at the 1971 Annual Meeting of the American Political Science Association).

41. Elizabeth and Anthony Leeds, "Brazil in the 1960's: Favelas and Polity: The Continuity of the Structure of Social Control."

42. See E. J. Hobsbawm, "Peasants and Rural Migrants in Politics," pp. 60 ff.

43. Oficina Nacional de Estadística y Censos, *Boletín de analisis demográfico*, Vol. 13: *Los pueblos jóvenes de Lima*, pp. 7 and 90.

44. Joan M. Nelson, "Sojourners vs. New Urbanites."

45. The hypothesis that settlement formation and government policy toward settlement formation encourage migration to the city is supported in another national context by Ray's work on Venezuela. He reports that "The revolution of January, 1958 ushered in a new and entirely unprecedented phase of barrio [settlement] development. Restrictions on land settlement were immediately lifted, and families poured out of their crowded ranchos to grab up vacant land on the outskirts of the cities as quickly as possible. When campesino families still in the countryside heard about the new opportunities, the flow of migration speeded up tremendously. . . ." See Talton F. Ray, *The Politics of the Barrios of Venezuela*, p. 32.

46. For a discussion of policies intended to encourage self-help among the urban poor, see Delgado, "Three Proposals." Charles M. Haar, in "Latin America's Troubled Cities," has discussed alternative policies, including policies to encourage private investment in housing.

47. For discussions of these alternative strategies see John Miller, "Channeling National Urban Growth in Latin America"; John Friedmann, "The Strategy of Deliberate Urbanization"; Peter R. Odell and David A. Preston, *Economies and Societies in Latin America: A Geographical Interpretation,* Chapter 5; and Lloyd Rodwin, *Nations and Cities: A Comparison of Strategies of Urban Growth.*

48. See Appendix II, Table II.3. These percentages were arrived at by combining the two columns in this table.

49. See *La Constitución del Perú,* p. 10; *Código de Minería,* Titles II and IX of Chapter I; and the *Reglamento General de Concesiones de Tierras y de Aguas Públicas para Irrigación* (in *Normas Legales: Revista de Legislación y Jurisprudencia,* Vol. 28, No. 1, 1958).

50. Kenneth A. Manaster, "The Problem of Urban Squatters in Developing Countries: Peru," pp. 29 and 38-39.

51. Kenneth L. Karst, *Latin American Legal Institutions,* pp. 471 ff.

52. William P. Glade, *The Latin American Economies,* p. 120.

53. See Article 16 of the *Reglamento General de Concesiones de Tierras y de Aguas Públicas para Irrigación.*

54. Suspicious fires of this type have been noted by Abrams in settlements in other parts of the world. See Abrams, *Man's Struggle for Shelter,* p. 22.

Chapter III

1. Charles Abrams, *Man's Struggle for Shelter in an Urbanizing World,* pp. 23-24.

2. See, for instance, José Matos Mar, "Migration and Urbanization—The Barriadas of Lima"; William Mangin, "Urbanization Case History in Peru," "Latin American Squatter Settlements," "Squatter Settlements"; Daniel Goldrich et al., "The Political Integration of Lower-Class Urban Settlements in Chile and Peru"; John F. C. Turner, "Barriers and Channels for Housing Development in Modernizing Countries."

3. See William Mangin, "Latin American Squatter Settlements," p. 69.

4. Mangin, "Urbanization Case History in Peru," p. 50.

5. Mangin, "Squatter Settlements," p. 23.

6. Turner, "Barriers and Channels," p. 171; and Henry A. Dietz, "Urban Squatter Settlements in Peru," p. 364.

7. Some caution is appropriate in dealing with the population data on squatter settlements. The number of families that actually participate in the initial formation of the settlement is usually small compared to the population of the settlement when it reaches its full size, often after many years of growth. In the analysis of the present total population of the settlements, I do not intend to imply that the government directly authorized the arrival of all of the families that arrived later on. Rather, one must think of the initial invasion (or authorization) as defining a particular area as being available for the formation of a new settlement and should note the present population of the settlement simply as a way of assessing how important a particular settlement (or period of formation) is in terms of the number of families to which it offered a new housing opportunity.

8. It is important to note that a somewhat larger proportion of the cases in the smaller sample involve government authorization—42 percent, instead of 30 percent (see Table 1). This results from the bias in the sample mentioned above toward getting the best information on cases that seemed most likely to be instances of government involvement.

9. See Appendix I.
10. See Appendix II, Table II.2.
11. See Appendix II, Tables II.3 and II.4.
12. See Appendix II, Table II.5.
13. See Appendix II, Table II.6.
14. See Appendix II, Table II.7.
15. See Appendix II, Tables II.9 and II.10.
16. Mangin, "Squatter Settlements," p. 23; and Carlos Delgado, *Tres Planteamientos en Torno a problemas de urbanización acelerada en areas metropolitanas*, p. 25.
17. Talton F. Ray, *The Politics of the Barrios of Venezuela*, pp. 31–32.
18. Ibid., pp. 32–33.
19. James L. Payne, *Labor and Politics in Peru*, p. 54.
20. The only apparent exception to this generalization might involve the *traficantes* referred to in Chapter V and others who at times acquire lots in settlements with the purpose of selling or renting them, rather than occupying them. However, these people could hardly be described as wealthy.
21. Theodore J. Lowi, "American Business, Public Policy, Case-Studies, and Political Theory," p. 690.
22. Ibid.
23. Ibid., pp. 697 ff.

Chapter IV

1. The first period of settlement policy considered in the analysis is thus also the first period in which there was a major role of the government in settlement formation. Detailed information on political involvement in settlement formation before 1945 is unfortunately hard to find, in part because few community leaders who were involved in the formation of these early settlements are still alive. However, as the data in the last chapter suggested, this was a period in which settlements were formed primarily through gradual occupation, with a few cases of invasions, and only two cases with clear evidence of government involvement. Both of these involved informal government intervention before the occupation of the land, and both occurred under military presidents, Sánchez Cerro and Benavides. There is also some evidence of involvement by Sánchez Cerro in preventing the eviction of another settlement after it was formed.
   It is noteworthy that both of these presidents came to power in the context of a major rivalry with the Apra party (see Frederick B. Pike, *The Modern History of Peru*, pp. 250 ff. and 268 ff.). Apra enjoyed strong mass support, and in part to compete with Apra's popularity, both Sánchez Cerro and Benavides also made major appeals for lower-class support (ibid., pp. 253 and 271). Though available information does not make it clear whether sponsoring these settlements was part of their effort to gain support, it was certainly consistent with it. As will be shown in this chapter, this same combination of military populism and anti-Aprismo was later to play a central role in the development of settlements in Lima.
2. Ibid., pp. 280 ff.
3. Ibid., pp. 280 and 283.
4. James L. Payne, *Labor and Politics in Peru*, p. 47.
5. Pike, *The Modern History*, pp. 284 ff.
6. Ibid., p. 286.
7. Ibid.
8. José Luis Bustamante y Rivero, *Tres años de lucha por la democracia en el Perú*, p. 109.
9. This enmity dates from a confrontation between Apra and the armed forces in the early 1930s. See Pike, *The Modern History*, pp. 265 ff. The following account is based on

information gathered in the survey of settlement formation and from interviews with party leaders, specialists in housing, and retired military and police officers.

10. Pike, *The Modern History*, p. 288.

11. François Bourricaud, "Structure and Function of the Peruvian Oligarchy," p. 26.

12. Víctor Villaneuva, *El militarismo en el Perú*, p. 123.

13. Bourricaud, "Structure and Function," p. 26.

14. Villanueva, *El militarismo*, p. 123.

15. Bustamante, *Tres años*, p. 264.

16. Pike, *The Modern History*, pp. 290–91.

17. Payne, *Labor and Politics*, pp. 50–51; and Pike, *The Modern History*, p. 291.

18. Payne, *Labor and Politics*, p. 51.

19. Percy MacLean y Estenós, *Historia de una revolución*, pp. 195–96 and 199–200.

20. François Bourricaud, "Lima en la vida política peruana," p. 94.

21. Pike, *The Modern History*, p. 291.

22. Ibid., p. 292.

23. MacLean, *Historia de una revolución*.

24. Ibid., p. 205.

25. See Law 11588 of 14 February 1951.

26. This name, which translates rather awkwardly into English, is typical for squatter settlement associations in Peru.

27. *La Prensa*, 17 August 1956, p. 5. The figure for the population of the settlement is close to that reported for the previous year in José Matos Mar, *Estudio de las barriadas limeñas*, p. 31.

28. Matos, *Estudio*, pp. 30–32.

29. *La Prensa*, 19 August 1956, p. 2.

30. Reports on these demonstrations and examples of the ads may be found scattered through *La Nación*, *La Prensa*, and *La Crónica* for most of the Odría period.

31. François Bourricaud, *Power and Society in Contemporary Peru*, p. 289.

32. John Duncan Powell, "Peasant Society and Clientelist Politics," pp. 423–24.

33. Ibid., p. 424.

34. Carlos A. Astiz, *Pressure Groups and Power Elites in Peruvian Politics*, p. 124, and personal interview with Víctor Villanueva and Julio de la Piedra.

35. Astiz, *Pressure Groups*, p. 124.

36. Pike, *The Modern History*, p. 292. The only significant departure from Odría's concentration of spending in Lima involved programs of public works in the Departments of Tacna, on the Chilean border, and Piura, on the Ecuadorian border (see Bourricaud, *Power and Society*, p. 290). Liisa North (personal communication) has suggested that these were initiated out of a concern with national security.

37. T. Paul Schultz, *Internal Migration*, pp. 30–31.

38. John Friedmann, "The Strategy of Deliberate Urbanization."

39. Albert O. Hirschman, "Policy-Making and Policy Analysis in Latin America—A Return Journey" (Paper presented at a Conference on the Comparative Analysis of Public Policy in Latin America, Buenos Aires, August 1974), p. 11.

Chapter V

1. Some discussion of the policy preferences of the export sector was presented in Chapter I. Jane S. Jaquette, "The Politics of Development in Peru," pp. 51–73, includes an extremely helpful analysis of these policy preferences. For a discussion of the conventional approach to development policy, see Charles W. Anderson, *Politics and Economic Change in Latin America*, pp. 163 ff. The reference to the laissez-faire approach as an "extreme" variant is on p. 163.

2. See Carlos Malpica, *Los dueños del Perú*, pp. 69 and 72.

3. Jaquette, "The Politics of Development," pp. 64–66.

4. Malpica, *Los dueños*, pp. 72 and 135.

5. Ibid., pp. 29, 191–92.

6. For a comment on this crossing over from the export sector to the urban sector with reference to Latin America more generally, see Guillermo A. O'Donnell, *Modernization and Bureaucratic-Authoritarianism*, p. 56.

7. Víctor Villanueva, *El militarismo en el Perú*, p. 127; José Luis Bustamante y Rivero, *Tres años de lucha par la democracia en el Perú*, pp. 308 ff.; and Carlos A. Astiz, *Pressure Groups and Power Elites in Peruvian Politics*, p. 139.

8. Villanueva, *El militarismo*, p. 124.

9. Frederick B. Pike, *The Modern History of Peru*, p. 291.

10. François Bourricaud, "Structure and Function of the Peruvian Oligarchy," p. 26; and Julio Cotler, "Political Crisis and Military Populism in Peru," pp. 95–96.

11. Villanueva, *El militarismo*, p. 133.

12. Astiz, *Pressure Groups*, p. 140.

13. See *Ultima Hora*, 28 November 1955, p. 9.

14. Cotler, "Political Crisis," pp. 95–96.

15. These arguments may be found in numerous editorials and articles in *La Prensa* during this period.

16. For examples, see the editorial page of *La Prensa* on 29 December 1954; 4 and 7 January 1955; 1 January, 29 March, and 10 October 1956; and 7 and 26 December 1957.

17. *La Prensa*, 7 December 1957, p. 8.

18. *La Prensa*, 1 January 1956, p. 3.

19. Comisión para la Reforma Agraria y la Vivienda, *Report on Housing in Peru*, p. 5.

20. *La Prensa*, 7 January 1955.

21. See *La Prensa*, 11 May 1961, p. 1.

22. *La Prensa*, 1 January 1956.

23. Pike, *The Modern History*, p. 290; and François Bourricaud, *Power and Society in Contemporary Peru*, pp. 290–91.

24. Pike, *The Modern History*, pp. 274 and 299.

25. Gordon Tullock, "The Charity of the Uncharitable."

26. For discussions of the question of definition of issues, see E. E. Schattschneider, *The Semisovereign People* (New York: Holt, Rinehart and Winston, 1960), p. 71; and Peter Bachrach and Morton Baratz, "The Two Faces of Power," pp. 947–52; and "Decisions and Nondecisions," pp. 632–42.

27. Albert O. Hirschman, *Journeys toward Progress*, pp. 301 ff.

28. See, for instance, *La Prensa*, 1 January 1956, p. 3.

29. *Caretas* X, No. 21 (22 December 1960 to 15 January 1961), p. 19. The quotation is part of an article that summarized the Social Progressive view of the housing problem.

30. Ibid. The Social Progressives admit on the same page of this article that Beltrán also recognized that underdevelopment and poverty were a problem. The difference obviously lay in the choice of which problem would be attacked by government policy. These issues were raised again by the newspaper *El Comercio* later in the same year. *El Comercio* was associated with urban banking and commercial interests and often criticized Beltrán's extreme position on free trade, as well as attacking the mutual funds, since they represented competition for Lima banks. As part of its attack on mutual funds, *El Comercio* pointed out that because of the problem of poverty, "the goal of everyone having their own home [*casa propia*] is fallacious; similarly, it is insincere to maintain that it will be possible to achieve this goal through the mutual savings and loan associations." See *El Comercio*, 25 October 1961, p. 3.

31. John F. C. Turner, "Barriers and Channels for Housing Development in Modernizing Countries," p. 167.

32. Comisión para la Reforma Agraria y la Vivienda, *Report on Housing*, Appendix 1.

33. Pike, *The Modern History*, p. 297; and Luis Dongo Denegri, *Vivienda y urbanismo*, pp. 172–73.

34. The Matos study was published as *Estudio de las barriadas limeñas* in 1966. See also Fondo Nacional de Salud y Bienestar Social, *Barriadas de Lima metropolitana, 1958–59;*

Adolfo Córdova V., *La vivienda en el Perú*; and Comisión para la Reforma Agraria y la Vivienda, *Report on Housing*.

35. *La Prensa*, 30 April 1959, p. 1.

36. The *Report on Housing* is the most important statement of Beltrán's policies. Discussions of these policies may be found starting in the early 1950s in *La Prensa*, both in news stories and on the editorial page. Data on his policies while prime minister may be found in sources such as his speech on housing before the Peruvian Senate, which was printed in its entirety in *La Prensa*, 7 October 1960.

37. Comisión para la Reforma Agraria y la Vivienda, *Report on Housing*, Chapter 7 and Appendix 4.

38. Ibid., Chapter 5.

39. Ibid., p. 38.

40. Ibid., Part 4.

41. Ibid., Appendix 1.

42. R. J. Owens, *Peru*, p. 59.

43. Guillermo Briones and José Mejía Valera, *El obrero industrial*, p. 71.

44. Comisión para la Reforma Agraria y la Vivienda, *Report on Housing*, Appendix 2, p. 206.

45. Ibid., p. 33.

46. Ibid., p. 77.

47. Ibid., p. 41.

48. Karl Marx, *The Eighteenth Brumaire of Louis Bonaparte*, p. 124.

49. Bourricaud, *Power and Society*, p. 325.

50. Comisión para la Reforma Agraria y la Vivienda, *Report on Housing*, Appendix 2, pp. 207–8.

51. Bourricaud, *Power and Society*, p. 325.

52. Comisión para la Reforma Agraria y la Vivienda, *Report on Housing*, Appendix 1, p. 203.

53. Ibid., Appendix 2, p. 208.

54. Ibid., Appendix 2, pp. 207–8.

55. Bourricaud, *Power and Society*, p. 326; and Ministerio de Agricultura, Dirección de Colonización, *Programa de Colonización de Quincemil (Cuzco)*. As with the housing programs, the efforts to encourage colonization during Beltrán's term as prime minister got extensive coverage in *La Prensa* and *Ultima Hora*. See, for instance, *La Prensa*, 31 October, 1959, p. 1; 15 November 1959, p. 9; 15 July 1960, p. 1; 14 February 1961, p. 1; 16 June 1962, p. 4; and *Ultima Hora*, 1 August 1960, p. 11.

Chapter VI

1. See François Bourricaud, *Power and Society in Contemporary Peru*, pp. 294 ff., and Frederick B. Pike, *The Modern History of Peru*, pp. 293 ff.

2. Pike, *The Modern History*, p. 299.

3. Charles W. Anderson, *Politics and Economic Change in Latin America*, pp. 174 ff.

4. G. S. Martínez, *Ley de barriadas*, pp. 51 ff.

5. The similarity is quite evident if one compares Law 13517 (described below) with Chapter 5 of the *Report on Housing in Peru*.

6. This interpretation, particularly regarding the role of Apra, was widely agreed upon among people interviewed who had followed the legislative developments during this period.

7. Luis Dongo Denegri, *Vivienda y urbanismo*, pp. 172–73.

8. Martínez, *Ley de barriadas*, pp. 110 ff.

9. Pike, *The Modern History*, p. 299.

10. Ibid., p. 300.

11. Ibid., p. 301.

12. Ibid., pp. 300–301; and Carlos Astiz, *Pressure Groups and Power Elites in Peruvian Politics*, pp. 146 ff.

13. Astiz, *Pressure Groups*, pp. 146 ff.

14. Pike, *The Modern History*, pp. 301–2.

15. Walter D. Harris et al., *Housing in Peru*, p. 568.

16. Astiz, *Pressure Groups*, p. 150.

17. Bourricaud, *Power and Society*, p. 319; and Astiz, *Pressure Groups*, pp. 149–50.

18. *La Prensa*, 19 August 1956, p. 2.

19. Pike, *The Modern History*, p. 307.

20. Ibid., pp. 308–9.

21. Ibid., p. 308.

22. Four architects interviewed by the author who had been closely familiar with Belaúnde's policies were in agreement on this point.

23. The following account relies on information from interviews with several architects who were familiar with JNV policy.

24. See Junta Nacional de la Vivienda, *Obra de la Junta Nacional de la Vivienda de julio de 1963 a octubre de 1967*.

25. Allan G. Austin and Sherman Lewis, *Urban Government for Metropolitan Lima*, pp. 47–48.

26. Law 16584 is included in Héctor E. Uchuya Reyes, ed., *Normas legales de pueblos jóvenes*, pp. 71–77.

27. See Supreme Decree 066-69-FO of 19 July 1968 (*La Crónica*, 20 July 1968, p. 3) and Supreme Decree 014-68-JC of 2 August 1968 (*El Peruano*, 5 August 1968, p. 7).

28. See Joan Nelson, "New Policies toward Squatter Settlements: Legalization versus Planners' Standards."

29. Comisión para la Reforma Agraria y la Vivienda, *Report on Housing in Peru*, p. 40.

30. In at least one case, this justification was evoked very much after the fact. The appearance of these settlements may be explained as much by the fact that these opposition parties controlled the local governments as by the fact that it was specifically legal under the terms of the *Reglamento*.

31. See Julio Cotler, "The Mechanics of Internal Domination and Social Change in Peru," pp. 238–40.

Chapter VII

1. The more important analyses of the origins and program of the military government that has ruled Peru since 1968 include Julio Cotler, "Political Crisis and Military Populism in Peru," pp. 95–113, and "Bases del corporativismo en el Perú," pp. 3–11; Jane S. Jaquette, "Revolution by Fiat: The Context of Policy-Making in Peru," pp. 648–67; James M. Malloy, "Authoritarianism, Corporatism, and Mobilization in Peru"; Abraham F. Lowenthal, ed., *The Peruvian Experiment* (Princeton: Princeton University Press, 1975); and Alfred Stepan, "State and Society: Peru in Comparative Perspective."

2. For a valuable discussion of this evolution in the orientation of the Peruvian military in the face of the crises of the 1960s, see Alfred Stepan, "State and Society," Chapter 4.

3. *La Prensa*, 7 November 1968, p. 4.

4. Ibid., 4 September 1972.

5. Decreto Supremo No. 105-68-FO. This is included in ONDEPJOV, *Documento Número 3*. The name was changed a few months after the decree from Organismo to Oficina.

6. ONDEPJOV, *Boletín Número 1*, p. 5.

7. Decreto Supremo No. 105-68-FO, in ONDEPJOV, *Documento Número 3*, p. 4.

8. This organizational arrangement is discussed in detail in Henry A. Dietz, "The Office and the Problador: Perceptions and Manipulations of Housing Authorities by the Lima Urban Poor," p. 15.

9. See *La Crónica,* 20 December 1968, p. 7.

10. Diego Robles, "El proceso de urbanización y los sectores populares," pp. 49–63. This article was written before the military government came to power.

11. See Carlos Delgado, *Tres planteamientos en torno a problemas de urbanización acelerada en areas metropolitanas: El caso de Lima.* Also published in English as "Three Proposals."

12. See ONDEPJOV, *Informe preliminar del censo, 1970,* pp. 5–6 and 37.

13. See *Encyclopedia of Associations,* p. 817.

14. ONDEPJOV, *Documento Número 3,* p. 1.

15. ONDEPJOV, *Boletín Número 1,* pp. 18–19.

16. ONDEPJOV, *Catálogo de instituciones de servico a la comunidad: Trujillo, Chimbote, Lima, y Arequipa.*

17. SINAMOS, Décima Región, *Dirigente vecinal,* back cover. This particular example is actually from the period after ONDEPJOV was absorbed in SINAMOS.

18. See John Strasma, "The United States and Agrarian Reform in Peru," p. 172.

19. Luigi R. Einaudi, "U.S. Relations with the Peruvian Military," pp. 22–23.

20. *El Peruano,* 4 October 1968.

21. See Marvin Alinsky, *Peruvian Political Perspective,* p. 4; and *Latin America* (weekly newsletter), 10 September 1971, pp. 293–94.

22. ONDEPJOV, *Documento Número 3,* p. 4.

23. *La Prensa,* 10 October 1969, p. 4.

24. Percy MacLean y Esteños, *Historia de una revolución,* p. 203.

25. See *La Prensa,* 28 February 1969, p. 1; 2 May 1969, p. 2; and 19 May 1969, p. 3; and *Expreso,* 26 May 1969, p. 3.

26. Einaudi, "U.S. Relations with the Peruvian Military," p. 27.

27. ONDEPJOV, *Documento Número 3,* p. 27.

28. *Expreso,* 23 May 1969, p. 10.

29. The rival, from Velarde's district of San Martin de Porras, was Alberto Díaz Jiménez. See *La Crónica,* 20 December 1968, p. 7.

30. Much of the information regarding the invasion is taken from Manuel Montoya, "El Pamplonazo." The newspaper clipping file of Henry Dietz was also a valuable aid in reconstructing the history of the invasion.

31. *La Prensa,* 12 May 1971.

32. Ibid.

33. *Correo,* 11 May and 18 May 1971.

34. Ibid., 15 May 1971, p. 14.

35. Ibid.

36. *Latin America,* 23 April 1971, pp. 129–30 and 11 June 1971, p. 186.

37. *El Peruano,* 24 June 1971, p. 5.

38. Ibid., Article 4c.

39. The regions of SINAMOS are described in the back of the official edition of the Organic Law of SINAMOS (Lima: 1972).

40. Ibid.

41. Ibid., p. 3.

42. See William Mangin, "Squatter Settlements," p. 25, for a comment on local democracy in the settlements.

43. See Title Five, *Disposiciones complementarias,* Number Six. Alfred Stepan called this interesting title to my attention.

44. See *Actualidad Militar* 11, No. 171 (January 1972), p. 30, and the 1972 official edition of the Organic Law, pp. 33–34.

45. SINAMOS, *Dirigente vecinal,* p. 3.

46. Reported by Alfred Stepan, personal communication.

47. *SINAMOS Informa,* Año 1, No. 1 (Lima: SINAMOS, Oficina Nacional de Difusión), p. 20.
48. *SINAMOS Informa,* Año 1, No. 2, pp. 29–32.
49. Alfred Stepan, personal communication.
50. *Decreto Ley* 18896, Article 5c.
51. See, for instance, *SINAMOS Informa,* Año 1, No. 2, p. 32 and *Expreso,* 1 October 1972, p. 1 (the latter with reference to Velasco's visit to the jungle).
52. *SINAMOS Informa,* Año 1, No. 1, p. 14.
53. Ibid., front cover.
54. Alfred Stepan, *The Military in Politics: Changing Patterns in Brazil,* p. 270.
55. See the discussion of plans for this settlement in *SINAMOS Informa,* Año 1, No. 2, pp. 29–32. The population figure was supplied by the SINAMOS office for the zone that includes Villa el Salvador.
56. *La Prensa,* 3 June 1972, p. 2.
57. There were almost daily articles in *La Prensa* and *El Comercio* during the first week of October 1972 on these invasions.
58. *El Comercio,* 13 November 1973.
59. *The Peruvian Times,* 6 July 1973.
60. Alfred Stepan, personal communication.
61. This was included in a mimeographed list of requirements which was available at local SINAMOS offices. Other personal documents and birth certificates for children were also required. In addition, the applicant had to be living on the lot and had to have a document showing that he did not own other real estate.
62. For a report on one of these mass marriages, see *La Prensa,* 19 December 1972.
63. See *La Prensa,* 14 September 1972, p. 7.
64. For a discussion of the government's plans for regional development, see John P. Robin and Frederick C. Terzo, *Urbanization in Peru* (New York: The Ford Foundation, 1973), pp. 25 ff.
65. See *La Prensa,* 2 November 1969, p. 1 (Chimbote), 1 June 1971 (Talara and Arequipa), and 25 August 1972 (Chiclayo).
66. These findings and this interpretation of the situation in provincial cities were supplied by Alfred Stepan.
67. See Maruja Acosta and Jorge E. Hardoy, *Reforma urbana en Cuba revolucionaria* (Caracas: Síntesis Dosmil, 1971), Chapters 5 and 6.
68. Information on this and several of the following points was supplied by Sinesio López.
69. See, for instance, *Oiga,* 8 November 1968, p. 13; 30 November 1968, p. 11; 21 March 1969; 11 April 1969; 12 September 1969, p. 14; and 16 November 1969. See also the *Declaración Política* published by the Christian Democrats in *Expreso,* 15 April 1973, p. 9.
70. *Oiga,* 9 November 1968, p. 13.
71. Ibid.
72. This is mentioned in most of the statements on urban reform cited above.
73. Oficina Nacional de Información, *Mensaje a la Nación,* 28 July 1969, pp. 13–14.
74. Ibid.
75. *El Comercio,* 3 September 1969, p. 3.
76. Ibid., 5 September 1969, p. 4.
77. *La Prensa,* 19 September 1969, p. 63.
78. Charles W. Anderson, *Politics and Economic Change in Latin America,* pp. 174 ff.
79. Ibid., pp. 183 ff.
80. Ibid., pp. 163 ff.
81. See Cotler, "Bases del corporativismo"; and Malloy, "Authoritarianism, Corporatism, and Mobilization."
82. Albert O. Hirschman, *Journeys toward Progress,* pp. 301 ff.
83. Theodore J. Lowi, "American Business, Public Policy, Case-Studies, and Political Theory," p. 695.

84. Ibid., p. 692.
85. Ibid.
86. Ibid., pp. 699–701.
87. This assessment is based on information gathered during a brief visit to Lima in August 1975. Henry Dietz kindly shared insights based on his own recent visit which confirmed and supplemented my principal conclusions.

Chapter VIII

1. See, for instance, Leonard Binder et al., *Crises and Sequences in Political Development*, and Gabriel A. Almond et al., eds., *Crises, Choice, and Change: Historical Studies of Political Development* (Boston: Little, Brown, 1973).

2. In concluding that the relationship between settlements and the political system depends on the political context, we are reaching the same conclusion that Joan Nelson has stated more broadly for the political consequences of urbanization. She suggests that the political orientations of lower-class, cityward migrants are influenced by various aspects of the political context. One crucial feature of the political context concerns which parties or other political groups reach the migrants most effectively. In Italy, the loyalty of cityward migrants was won by a well-organized Communist party, which was highly sensitive to their needs and problems (Joan M. Nelson, *Migrants, Urban Poverty, and Instability in Developing Nations*, pp. 24–25 and 69–70). In Peru, by contrast, it was the political right that most effectively responded to the needs of migrants.

3. See Peter S. Cleaves, *Bureaucratic Politics and Administration in Chile*, Chapter 8.

4. Susan Eckstein, personal communication.

5. Elizabeth and Anthony Leeds, "Brazil in the 1960s: Favelas and Polity"; Talton F. Ray, *The Politics of the Barrios of Venezuela*, p. 32; Joan M. Nelson, "New Policies Toward Squatter Settlements"; and Michael A. Cohen, *Urban Policy and Political Conflict in Africa: A Study of the Ivory Coast*.

6. Personal communication from Richard E. Stryker.

7. Guillermo A. O'Donnell, *Modernization and Bureaucratic-Authoritarianism*.

8. Frances Fox Piven and Richard A. Cloward, *Regulating the Poor*.

9. For a discussion of these stages that focuses particularly on Britain, France, and also on the United States, see Gaston V. Rimlinger, *Welfare Policy and Industrialization in Europe, America, and Russia*, Chapters 2 and 3 and Part 2. For a parallel discussion of stages, see Alva Myrdal, *Nation and Family: The Swedish Experiment in Democratic Family and Population Policy* (Cambridge, Mass.: M.I.T. Press, 1968), p. 152.

10. Rimlinger, *Welfare Policy*, pp. 32–33.

11. Ibid., Chapter 3.

12. Ibid., pp. 39–40 and 48. For a discussion of the Victorian approach to charity and self-help, see also José Nun, *Latin America*, p. 43.

13. Charles W. Anderson, *Politics and Economic Change in Latin America*, p. 104.

14. For an interesting discussion with reference to the United States of the significance of the formality of the commitments of social security programs for political legitimacy, see Theodore J. Lowi, *The End of Liberalism*, pp. 223–26.

15. For an attempt to conceptualize modernization in these terms and to derive and test cross-nationally hypotheses about the consequences of diffusion for the process of modernization, see my "Timing of Economic Growth and Regime Characteristics in Latin America," *Comparative Politics* 7, No. 3 (April 1975), pp. 331–59; and also David Collier and Richard E. Messick, "Prerequisites versus Diffusion: Testing Alternative Explanations of Social Security Adoption," *American Political Science Review* 69, No. 4 (December 1975). These articles cite and review a substantial body of literature dealing with these issues.

16. The point is obviously not that alternative models of settlement policy itself were diffused to Peru, but rather that the appearance of the basic approaches to linking the poor to the state that flow from classical liberalism and from the emergence of competitive party systems must be understood in part in terms of diffusion.

17. See A. F. K. Organski, *The Stages of Political Development*, p. 160.

18. For a discussion of this consequence with reference to social security in Latin America, see Collier and Messick, "Prerequisites versus Diffusion."

Appendix I

1. The published sources that were particularly helpful were José Matos Mar, *Estudio de las barriadas limeñas;* Fondo Nacional de Salud y Bienestar Social, *Barriadas de Lima metropolitana, 1958-59*; and Carlos Enrique Paz Soldán, *Lima y sus suburbios*. The archives of the Oficina de Barrios Marginales of the Junta Nacional de la Vivienda and the Newspaper Clipping Archive of *La Prensa* were particularly valuable sources of data.

2. Oficina Nacional de Desarrollo de Pueblos Jóvenes, *Informe preliminar del censo, 1970.*

Selected Bibliography

Abrams, Charles. *Man's Struggle for Shelter in an Urbanizing World.* Cambridge: M.I.T. Press, 1964.

Alberti, Giorgio. "The Breakdown of Provincial Urban Power Structure and the Rise of Peasant Movements." *Proceedings of the Third World Congress for Rural Sociology,* Baton Rouge, Louisiana, 1972. Assen, the Netherlands: Van Goncum, 1972.

Alers, J. Oscar, and Richard P. Appelbaum. "La migración en el Perú: Un inventario de proposiciones." Lima: Centro de Estudios de Población y Desarrollo, *Estudios de Población y Desarrollo I,* No. 4 (1968).

Alexander, R. Alberto. *Estudio sobre la crisis de la habitación en Lima.* Lima: Imprenta Torres Aguirre, 1922.

Alinsky, Marvin. *Peruvian Political Perspective.* Tempe: Center for Latin American Studies, Arizona State University, 1972.

Almond, Gabriel A., et al., eds. *Crisis, Choice, and Change: Historical Studies of Political Development.* Boston: Little, Brown, 1973.

Anderson, Bo, and James D. Cockroft. "Control and Coöptation in Mexican Politics." Pp. 366–89 in Irving Louis Horowitz, ed., *Radicalism in Latin America.* New York: Vintage Books, 1969.

Anderson, Charles W. *Politics and Economic Change in Latin America: The Governing of Restless Nations.* Princeton: D. Van Nostrand Co., 1967.

Andrews, Frank M., and George W. Phillips. "The Squatters of Lima: Who They Are and What They Want." *Journal of Developing Areas* IV, No. 2 (January 1970), 211–24.

Antonini, Gustavo A., ed. *Public Policy and Urbanization in the Dominican Republic and Costa Rica.* Gainesville: Center for Latin American Studies, University of Florida, 1973.

Arca Parró, A. "La ciudad capital de la república y el censo nacional de 1940." *Estadística Peruana,* Año 1, No. 1. Lima: 1945.

Astiz, Carlos A. *Pressure Groups and Power Elites in Peruvian Politics.* Ithaca: Cornell University Press, 1969.

169

Austin, Allan G., and Sherman Lewis. *Urban Government for Metropolitan Lima.* New York: Praeger Publishers, 1970.

Bachmura, Frank T. "Urbanization as an Alternative to Land Reform." Washington, D.C.: Agency for International Development, *Spring Review of Land Reform,* SR/LR/A5 (June 1970).

Bachrach, Peter, and Morton Baratz. "Decisions and Nondecisions: An Analytical Framework." *American Political Science Review* XLVII (September 1963), 632–42.

———. "The Two Faces of Power." *American Political Science Review* XLVI (December 1962), pp. 947–52.

Banks, Arthur S. *Cross-Polity Time-Series Data.* Cambridge: M.I.T. Press, 1971.

Berckholtz Salinas, Pablo. *Barrios marginales: Aberración social.* Lima: 1963.

Binder, Leonard, et al., *Crises and Sequences in Political Development.* Princeton: Princeton University Press, 1971.

Bourricaud, François. "Lima en la vida política peruana." *América Latina* (Rio de Janeiro) VII, No. 4 (October-December 1964), 89–95.

———. *Power and Society in Contemporary Peru.* Translated by Paul Stevenson. New York: Praeger, 1970.

———. "Structure and Function of the Peruvian Oligarchy." *Studies in Comparative International Development* II, No. 2 (1966), 17–36.

Briones, Guillermo, and José Mejía Valera. *El obrero industrial.* Lima: Universidad Nacional Mayor de San Marcos, Instituto de Investigaciones Sociológicas, 1964.

Bureau of Social Affairs of the United Nations. "Some Policy Implications of Urbanization." Pp. 294–324 in Philip M. Hauser, ed., *Urbanization in Latin America.* New York: Columbia University Press, International Documents Service, 1961.

Bustamante y Rivero, José Luis. *Tres Años de lucha por la democracia en el Perú.* Buenos Aires: Bartolomé U. Chiesino, 1949.

Campbell, Donald T., and Julian C. Stanley. *Experimental and Quasi-Experimental Designs for Research.* Chicago: Rand McNally, 1963.

Caravedo, Baltazar, Humberto Rotondo, and Javier Mariategui. *Estudios de psiquiatría social en el Perú.* Lima: Ediciones del Sol, 1963.

Cardoso, Fernando Henrique, and Enzo Faletto. *Dependencia y desarrollo en América Latina: Ensayo de interpretación sociológica.* Mexico City: Siglo Veintiuno Editores, 1969.

Centro de Investigaciones Sociales por Muestreo. *Barriadas de Lima: Actitudes de los habitantes respecto a servicios públicos y privados.* Lima: Ministerio de Trabajo y Comunidades, Servicio del Empleo y Recursos Humanos, 1967.

Chaplin, David. *The Peruvian Industrial Labor Force.* Princeton: Princeton University Press, 1967.

Cleaves, Peter S. *Bureaucratic Politics and Administration in Chile.* Berkeley and Los Angeles: University of California Press, 1974.

Código de Minería. Lima: Editorial Mercurio, N.D.

Cohen, Michael A. *Urban Policy and Political Conflict in Africa: A Study of the Ivory Coast.* Chicago: University of Chicago Press, 1974.

Comisión para la Reforma Agraria y la Vivienda. *Report on Housing in Peru.* Mexico City: Regional Technical Aids Center, International Cooperation Administration, 1959.

La Constitución del Perú. Lima: Editorial Juan Mejía Baca, 1958.

Córdova V., Adolfo. *La vivienda en el Perú: Estado actual y evaluación de las necesidades.* Lima: Casa de la Moneda, 1958.

Cornelius, Wayne A., Jr. "The Political Sociology of Cityward Migration in Latin America: Toward Empirical Theory." Pp. 95-147 in Francine F. Rabinovitz and Felicity M. Trueblood, eds. *Latin American Urban Research.* Beverly Hills: Sage Publications, 1971.

―――. "Urbanization and Political Demand Making: Political Participation Among the Migrant Poor in Latin American Cities." *American Political Science Review* LXVIII, No. 3 (September 1974), 1125-46.

Cornelius, Wayne A., and Henry A. Dietz. "Urbanization, Demand-Making, and Political System Overload: Political Participation among the Migrant Poor in Latin American Cities." Paper presented at the 1973 Annual Meeting of the American Political Science Association, New Orleans.

Corporación Nacional de la Vivienda. *Experiencias relativas de la vivienda de interés social en el Perú.* Lima: 1958.

Cotler, Julio. "Bases del corporativismo en el Perú." *Sociedad y política* 2, No. 1 (October 1972), 3-11.

―――. "Estructura social y urbanización: Algunas notas comparativas." Lima: Instituto de Estudios Peruanos, Documentos Teóricos No. 3, 1967.

―――. "The Mechanics of Internal Domination and Social Change in Peru." *Studies in Comparative International Development* III, No. 12 (1967-68), 229-46.

―――. "Political Crisis and Military Populism in Peru." *Studies in Comparative International Development* VI, No. 5 (1970-71), 95-113.

―――. "Traditional Haciendas and Communities in a Context of Political Mobilization in Peru." Pp. 533-58 in Rodolfo Stavenhagen, ed., *Agrarian Problems and Peasant Movements in Latin America.* Garden City, N.Y.: Anchor Books, 1970.

Davies, James C. "Toward a Theory of Revolution." *American Sociological Review* XXVII, No. 1 (February 1962), 5-19.

Davis, Kingsley. *World Urbanization 1950-1970,* Vol. I: *Basic Data for Cities, Countries, and Regions.* Population Monograph Series No. 4, Berkeley: Institute of International Studies, University of California, 1969.

Delgado, Carlos. *Tres planteamientos en torno a problemas de urbanización acelerada en areas metropolitanas: El caso de Lima.* Lima: Cuadernos PLAN-DEMET, Serie Anaranjada, Asuntos Sociales No. 1, 1968. Also published as "Three Proposals Regarding Accelerated Urbanization Problems in Metropolitan Areas: The Lima Case." Pp. 269-311 in John Miller and Ralph A. Gakenheimer, eds., *Latin American Urban Policies and the Social Sciences.* Beverly Hills: Sage Publications, 1971.

Dietz, Henry A. "Becoming A Poblador: Political Adjustment to the Urban Environment in Lima, Peru." Ph.D. dissertation, Department of Political Science, Stanford University, 1974.

―――. "The Office and the Poblador: Perceptions and Manipulations of Housing Authorities by the Lima Urban Poor." Paper presented at the 1973 Annual Meeting of the American Society for Public Administration.

―――. "Urban Squatter Settlements in Peru: A Case History and Analysis." *Journal of Inter-American Studies* XI, No. 3 (July 1969), 353-70.

Dirección de Estadística. *Resúmenes del censo de las provincias de Lima y Callao de 1920.* Lima: 1927.

Dirección Nacional de Estadística. *Censo nacional de población y ocupación de 1940.* Lima: 1944.

―――. *Encuesta de inmigración: Lima metropolitana.* Lima: 1968.

―――. *Sexto censo nacional de población: Centros poblados*, Tomo 3. Lima: 1966.

Dirección de Salubridad Pública. *Censo de la provincia de Lima de 1908.* Lima: 1915.

Dongo Denegri, Luis. *Vivienda y urbanismo.* Arequipa: Editorial el Deber, 1962.

Dorich, Luis T. "Urbanization and Physical Planning in Peru." Pp. 280–93 in Philip M. Hauser, ed., *Urbanization in Latin America.* New York: Columbia University Press, International Documents Service, 1961.

Eckstein, Harry. *Pressure Group Politics.* Stanford: Stanford University Press, 1960.

Eckstein, Susan. "Theory and Methods in the Study of Poverty and the Politics of Poverty: The Substitution of a Social-Economic Structural Approach for an Individualistic Cultural Approach." Paper presented at the 1971 Annual Meeting of the American Political Science Association, Chicago.

Einaudi, Luigi R. *The Peruvian Military: A Summary Political Analysis.* Rand Corporation Memorandum RM-6048-RC, 1969.

―――. "U.S. Relations with the Peruvian Military." Pp. 15–56 in Daniel A. Sharp, ed., *U.S. Foreign Policy and Peru.* Austin: University of Texas Press, 1972.

Encyclopedia of Associations. 7th ed. Detroit: Gale Research Co., 1972.

Fondo Nacional de Salud y Bienestar Social. *Barriadas de Lima metropolitana, 1958–59.* Lima: 1960.

Ford, Thomas R. *Man and Land in Peru.* Gainesville: University of Florida Press, 1962.

Freeman, Linton C. *Elementary Applied Statistics.* New York: John Wiley, 1965.

Friedmann, John. "The Strategy of Deliberate Urbanization." *Journal of the American Institute of Planners* XXXIV, No. 6 (November 1968), 364–73.

Germani, Gino. "Emigración del campo a la ciudad y sus causas." Pp. 71-90 in Horacio Giberti et al., eds., *Sociedad, economía, y reforma agraria.* Buenos Aires: Ediciones Libera, 1959.

Gianella, Jaime. *Marginalidad en Lima metropolitana.* Lima: Centro de Estudios y Promoción de Desarrollo, 1970.

Glade, William P. *The Latin American Economies.* New York: American Book Co., 1969.

Goldrich, Daniel et al. "The Political Integration of Lower-Class Urban Settlements in Chile and Peru." *Studies in Comparative International Development* III, No. 1 (1967–68), 1–22.

Gómez, Rudolph. *The Peruvian Administrative System.* Boulder: University of Colorado, Bureau of Government Research, 1969.

Goulet, Denis, and Michael Hudson. *The Myth of Aid.* Maryknoll, N.Y.: Orbis Books, 1971.

Gutierrez Vidalon, Hugo. "Tugurio: Estudio de casos." Lima: PLANDEMET, Oficina de Relaciones Públicas, 1969.

Haar, Charles M. "Latin America's Troubled Cities." *Foreign Affairs* XLI, No. 3 (April 1963), 536–49.

Harris, Walter D. et al. *Housing in Peru.* Washington: Pan American Union, 1963.

Hayter, Teresa. *Aid as Imperialism.* Penguin Books, 1971.
Hirschman, Albert O. *Journeys toward Progress.* Garden City, N.Y.: Anchor Books, 1965.
Hobsbawm, E.J. "Peasants and Rural Migrants in Politics." Pp. 43–65 in Claudio Véliz, ed., *The Politics of Conformity.* New York: Oxford University Press, 1970.
Huntington, Samuel P. *Political Order in Changing Societies.* New Haven: Yale University Press, 1968.
Instituto de Estudios Peruanos. *La oligarquía en el Perú.* Lima: Moncloa Campodónico, 1969.
Instituto Nacional de Planificación. *Plan de desarrollo económico y social 1967–70: Plan sectorial de vivienda.* Lima: N.D.
Jacobs, Jane. *The Death and Life of Great American Cities.* New York: Vintage Books, 1961.
Jaquette, Jane S. "The Politics of Development in Peru." Ph.D. dissertation, Department of Government, Cornell University, 1971.
———. "Revolution by Fiat: The Context of Policy Making in Peru." *Western Political Quarterly* XXV (December 1972), 648–67.
Johnson, John J. *Political Change in Latin America: The Emergence of the Middle Sectors.* Stanford: Stanford University Press, 1958.
Junta Departamental Pro-desocupados. *Censo de las provincias de Lima y Callao en 1931.* Lima: 1931.
Junta Nacional de la Vivienda. *Obra de la Junta Nacional de la Vivienda de julio de 1963 a octubre de 1967.* Lima: N.D.
Karst, Kenneth L. *Latin American Legal Institutions.* Los Angeles: Latin American Center, University of California, 1966.
Klarén, Peter F. *Modernization, Dislocation, and Aprismo: Origins of the Peruvian Aprista Party, 1870–1932.* Austin: University of Texas Press, 1973.
Kornhauser, William. *The Politics of Mass Society.* Glencoe: The Free Press, 1959.
Lambert, Jacques. *Latin America.* Translated by Helen Katel. Berkeley and Los Angeles: University of California Press, 1967.
Larson, Magali Sarfatti, and Arlene Eisen Bergman. *Social Stratification in Peru.* Berkeley: Institute of International Studies, University of California, Politics of Modernization Series No. 5, 1969.
Lazarsfeld, Paul F. "Interpretation of Statistical Relations as a Research Operation." Pp. 115–24 in Paul F. Lazarsfeld and Morris Rosenberg, eds., *The Language of Social Research.* (New York: The Free Press, 1955).
Leeds, Elizabeth, and Anthony Leeds. "Brazil in the 1960's: Favelas and Polity, the Continuity of the Structure of Social Control." LADAC Occasional Papers (Institute of Latin American Studies, University of Texas, Austin), Series 2, No. 5.
Lewis, Oscar. "Further Observations on the Folk-Urban Continuum and Urbanization with Special Reference to Mexico City." Pp. 491–503 in Philip M. Hauser and Leo F. Schnore, eds., *The Study of Urbanization.* New York: John Wiley, 1965.
———. "Urbanization without Breakdown: A Case Study." *Scientific Monthly* LXXV (July 1952), 31–41.
Linz, Juan J. "An Authoritarian Regime: Spain." Pp. 291–341 in Erik Allardt and Yrjo Littunen, eds., *Cleavages, Ideologies, and Party Systems.* Transactions of the Westermarck Society 10. Helsinki: Academic Bookstore, 1964.

———. "Notes toward a Typology of Authoritarian Regimes." Paper presented at the 1972 Annual Meeting of the American Political Science Association, Chicago.

———. "Totalitarian and Authoritarian Regimes." In Fred Greenstein and Nelson Polsby, eds., *Handbook of Political Science*. Reading, Mass.: Addison-Wesley, 1975.

Lowi, Theodore J. "American Business, Public Policy, Case-Studies, and Political Theory." *World Politics* XVI, No. 4 (July 1964), 677–715.

———. "Decision Making vs. Policy Making: Toward an Antidote for Technocracy." *Public Administration Review* XXX, No. 3 (May–June 1970), 314–25.

———. *The End of Liberalism*. New York: W.W. Norton, 1969.

———. "Four Systems of Policy, Politics, and Choice." *Public Administration Review* XXXII, No. 4 (July–August 1972), 298–310.

MacDonald, J.S. "Agricultural Organization, Migration, and Labour Militancy in Rural Italy." *Economic History Review* XVI, No. 1 (1963), 61–75.

MacLean y Estenós, Percy. *Historia de una revolución*. Buenos Aires: Editorial E.A.P.A.L., 1953.

Malloy, James M. "Authoritarianism, Corporatism, and Mobilization in Peru." *The Review of Politics* 36, No. 1 (January 1974), 52–84.

Malpica, Carlos. *Los dueños del Perú*. Lima: Ediciones Ensayos Sociales, 1968.

———. *El Mito de la ayuda exterior*. Lima: Francisco Moncloa Editores, 1967.

Manaster, Kenneth A. "The Problem of Urban Squatters in Developing Countries: Peru." *Wisconsin Law Review* I (1968), 23–61.

———. "Squatters and the Law: The Relevance of the United States' Experience to Current Problems in the Developing Countries." *Tulane Law Review* XLIII, No. 1 (December 1968), 94–127.

Mangin, William. "Latin American Squatter Settlements: A Problem and a Solution." *Latin American Research Review* II, No. 3 (Summer 1967), 65–98.

———. "Mental Health and Migration to Cities: A Peruvian Case." Pp. 545–55 in D.B. Heath and R.N. Adams, eds., *Contemporary Cultures and Societies of Latin America*. New York: Random House, 1965.

———. "The Role of Regional Associations in the Adaptation of Rural Migrants to Cities in Peru." Pp. 311–23 in D.B. Heath and R.N. Adams, eds., *Contemporary Cultures and Societies of Latin America*. New York: Random House, 1965.

———. "Squatter Settlements." *Scientific American* CCXVII, No. 4 (October 1967), 21–29.

———. "Urbanization Case History in Peru." *Architectural Design* VIII (August 1963), 366–70.

Mangin, William, and Jerome Cohen. "Cultural and Psychological Characteristics of Mountain Migrants to Lima." *Sociologus* XIV, No. 1 (1965), 81–88.

Martínez, G. S. *Ley de barriadas*. Lima: Distribuidora Bendezu, 1965.

Martínez, Héctor. "Las migraciones internas en el Perú." *Estudios de Población y Desarrollo* II, No. 1 (1968).

Marx, Karl. *The Eighteenth Brumaire of Louis Bonaparte*. New York: International Publishers, 1963.

Matos Mar, José. *Estudio de las barriadas limeñas*. Lima: Departamento de Antropología, Universidad Nacional Mayor de San Marcos, 1967.

———. "Migration and Urbanization—The 'Barriadas' of Lima: An Example of Integration into Urban Life," pp. 170–90 in Philip M. Hauser, ed., *Urbaniza-*

tion in Latin America. New York: Columbia University Press, International Documents Service, 1961.

Merrill, Robert North. "Toward a Structural Housing Policy: An Analysis of Chile's Low Income Housing Program." Ph.D. dissertation, Cornell University, 1971.

Michl, Sara. "Urban Squatter Organization as a National Government Tool: The Case of Lima, Peru." Pp. 155–80 in Francine F. Rabinovitz and Felicity M. Trueblood, eds., *Latin American Urban Research,* Vol. 3. Beverly Hills: Sage Publications, 1973.

Miller, John. "Channeling National Urban Growth in Latin America." Pp. 107–66 in John Miller and Ralph A. Gakenheimer, eds., *Latin American Urban Policies and the Social Sciences.* Beverly Hills: Sage Publications, 1971.

Ministerio de Agricultura. Dirección de Colonización, *Programa de Colonización de Quincemil (Cuzco).* Lima: 1962.

Montoya, Manuel, "El Pamplonazo." Dissertation, Department of Sociology, San Marcos University, 1972.

Moore, Barrington, Jr. *Social Origins of Dictatorship and Democracy: Lord and Peasant in the Making of the Modern World.* Boston: Beacon Press, 1966.

Morse, Richard M. "The Heritage of Latin America." Pp. 123–77 in Louis Hartz, ed., *The Founding of New Societies.* New York: Harcourt, Brace and World, 1964.

Needler, Martin C. *Political Development in Latin America.* New York: Random House, 1968.

Nelson, Joan M. *Migrants, Urban Poverty, and Instability in Developing Nations.* Cambridge: Center for International Affairs, Harvard University, Occasional Papers in International Affairs No. 22, 1969.

_____. "New Policies toward Squatter Settlements: Legalization versus Traditional Planners' Standards." Unpublished manuscript.

_____. "Sojourners vs. New Urbanites: Causes and Consequences of Temporary vs. Permanent Cityward Migration in Developing Countries." Unpublished manuscript.

Nordlinger, Eric. "Time Sequences and Rates of Change," *World Politics* 20, No. 3 (April 1968), pp. 494–520.

North, Liisa. "Origins and Development of the Peruvian Apra Party." Ph.D. dissertation, Department of Political Science, University of California at Berkeley, 1973.

Nun, José. *Latin America: The Hegemonic Crisis and the Military Coup.* Berkeley: Institute of International Studies, University of California, Politics of Modernization Series No. 7, 1969.

Odell, Peter R. and David A. Preston. *Economies and Societies in Latin America: A Geographical Interpretation.* New York: John Wiley, 1973.

O'Donnell, Guillermo A. "Estado y corporativismo en América Latina," in James M. Malloy, ed., *Authoritarianism and Corporatism in Latin America.* Pittsburgh: University of Pittsburgh Press, forthcoming.

_____. *Modernization and Bureaucratic-Authoritarianism: Studies in South American Politics.* Berkeley: Institute of International Studies, University of California, Politics of Modernization Series No. 9, 1973.

Oficina Nacional de Desarrollo de Pueblos Jóvenes. *Boletín Número 1.* Lima: 1969.

_____. *Catálogo de instituciones de servicio a la comunidad: Trujillo, Chimbote, Lima, y Arequipa.* Lima: 1971.

_____. *Documento Número 3*. Lima: 1969.

_____. *Informe preliminar del censo, 1970*. Lima: 1971.

Oficina Nacional de Estadística y Censos. *Boletín de analysis demográfico*, Vol. 13: *Los pueblos jóvenes de Lima*. Lima: 1972.

Oficina Nacional de Información. *Mensaje a la Nación*, 28 July, 1969. Lima: 1969.

Orbell, John M., and Toru Uno. "A Theory of Neighborhood Problem Solving: Political Action vs. Residential Mobility." *American Political Science Review* LXVI, No. 2 (June 1972), 471–89.

Organski, A.F.K. *The Stages of Political Development*. New York: Alfred A. Knopf, 1965.

Owens, R.J. *Peru*. London: Oxford University Press, 1963.

Paige, Glenn D. "The Rediscovery of Politics." Pp. 49–58 in John D. Montgomery and William J. Siffin, eds., *Approaches to Development: Politics, Administration, and Change*. New York: McGraw-Hill, 1966.

Patch, Richard. "La Parada, Lima's Market." *American Universities Field Staff Reports, West Coast South America Series* XIV, Nos. 1–3 (1967).

_____. "Life in a Callejón: A Study of Urban Disorganization." *American Universities Field Staff Reports, West Coast South America Series* VIII, No. 6 (June 1961).

_____. "The Peruvian Elections of 1963." Pp. 498–513 in Robert D. Tomasek, ed., *Latin American Politics*. Garden City, N.Y.: Doubleday, 1966.

Payne, James L. *Labor and Politics in Peru*. New Haven: Yale University Press, 1965.

_____. "The Oligarchy Muddle." *World Politics* XX, No. 3 (April 1968), 439–53.

Paz Soldán, Carlos Enrique. *Lima y sus suburbios*. Lima: Universidad Nacional Mayor de San Marcos, Biblioteca de Cultura Sanitaria, Instituto de Medicina Social, 1957.

Perlman, Janice Elaine. "The Fate of Migrants in Rio's Favelas: Portrait of the People." Paper presented at a Conference on Recent Research on Rural-Urban Migration, M.I.T., 1971.

Petras, James. *Politics and Social Forces in Chile*. Berkeley and Los Angeles: University of California Press, 1970.

Phelan, John Leddy, "Authority and Flexibility in the Spanish Imperial Bureaucracy," *Administrative Science Quarterly* 5, No. 1 (June 1960), 47–65.

Pike, Fredrick B. *The Modern History of Peru*. New York: Praeger, 1967.

Piven, Frances Fox, and Richard A. Cloward. *Regulating the Poor: The Functions of Public Welfare*. New York: Pantheon Press, 1971.

PLANDEMET. *Estudio de tugurios en los distritos de Jesús María y la Victoria*. Lima: Plan de Desarrollo Metropolitano Lima-Callao, 1968.

Powell, John Duncan. "Peasant Society and Clientelist Politics." *American Political Science Review* LXIV, No. 2 (June 1970), 411–25.

Powell, Sandra. "Political Participation in the Barriadas: A Case Study." *Comparative Political Studies* II, No. 2 (July 1969), 195–215.

Presidencia de la República. Sistema Nacional de Apoyo a la Movilización Social. *Ley Organica*. Lima: 1972.

Quijano, Aníbal. "Urbanización y tendencias de cambio en la sociedad rural en latinoamérica." Lima: Instituto de Estudios Peruanos. Documentos Teóricos No. 5, 1967.

Ray, Talton F. *The Politics of the Barrios of Venezuela*. Berkeley and Los Angeles: University of California Press, 1969.

Redfield, Robert. "The Folk Society." *American Journal of Sociology* LII (January 1947), 293–308.

Rimlinger, Gaston V. *Welfare Policy and Industrialization in Europe, America, and Russia.* New York: John Wiley, 1971.

Robles, Diego. "El proceso de urbanización y los sectores populares." Cuadernos DESCO (February 1969).

Rodwin, Lloyd. *Nations and Cities: A Comparison of Strategies of Urban Growth.* Boston: Houghton Mifflin, 1970.

Rotondo, Humberto. "Psychological and Mental Health Problems of Urbanization Based on Case Studies in Peru." Pp. 249–57 in Philip M. Hauser, ed., *Urbanization in Latin America.* New York: Columbia University Press, International Documents Service, 1961.

Schmitter, Philippe C. *Interest Conflict and Political Change in Brazil,* Stanford: Stanford University Press, 1971.

————. "Paths to Political Development in Latin America." Pp. 83–105 in Douglas A. Chalmers, ed., *Changing Latin America: New Interpretations of its Politics and Society.* Proceedings of the Academy of Political Science, Columbia University, Vol. 30, No. 4 (August 1972).

Schoultz, Lars. "Urbanization and Political Change in Latin America." *Midwest Journal of Political Science* XVI (August 1972), 367–87.

Schultz, T. Paul. *Internal Migration: A Quantitative Study of Rural-Urban Migration in Colombia.* Rand Corporation Document P-3905-1, 1969.

Sistema Nacional de Apoyo a la Movilización Social Décima Región. *Dirigente vecinal.* Lima: 1972.

Stepan, Alfred. *The Military in Politics: Changing Patterns in Brazil.* Princeton: Princeton University Press, 1971.

————. "State and Society: Peru in Comparative Perspective." Unpublished manuscript, Department of Political Science, Yale University.

Stokes, Charles. "A Theory of Slums." *Land Economics* XXXVIII, No. 3 (August 1962), 187–97.

Strasma, John. "The United States and Agrarian Reform in Peru." Pp. 156–205 in Daniel A. Sharp, ed., *U.S. Foreign Policy and Peru.* Austin: University of Texas Press, 1972.

Tullock, Gordon. "The Charity of the Uncharitable." Paper presented at the 1971 Annual Meeting of the American Political Science Association, Chicago.

Turner, John F.C. "Barriers and Channels for Housing Development in Modernizing Countries." *Journal of the American Institute of Planners* XXXII, No. 3 (May 1967), 167–81.

————. "Uncontrolled Urban Settlement: Problems and Policies." *International Social Development Review* (United Nations), No. 1 (1968), 107–30.

————. "Lima Barriadas Today." *Architectural Design* (London) XXXIII, No. 8 (1963), 369–80, 389–93.

————. "Lima's *Barriadas* and *Corralones*: Suburbs vs. Slums." *Ekistics* (Greece) XIX, No. 112 (1965), 152–56.

Uchuya Reyes, Héctor E., ed. *Normas legales de pueblos jóvenes.* Lima: Ediciones Heur, 1971.

Villanueva, Víctor. *El militarismo en el Perú.* Lima: Empresa Gráfica T. Scheuch, 1962.

Whyte, William Foote. *Street Corner Society.* Chicago: University of Chicago Press, 1943.

Wiarda, Howard J. "Toward a Framework for the Study of Political Change in the Iberic-Latin Tradition: The Corporative Model," *World Politics* 25, No. 2 (January 1973), 206–35.

Wirth, Louis. "Urbanism as a Way of Life." *American Journal of Sociology* XLIV (July 1938), 1–24.

Wolfe, Marshall. "Social Security and Development: The Latin American Experience." Pp. 155–86 in Everett M. Kassalow, ed., *The Role of Social Security in Economic Development.* Washington, D.C.: U.S. Department of Health, Education, and Welfare, Social Security Administration, Research Report No. 27, 1968.

Zeldin, Theodore. *The Political System of Napoleon III.* London: Macmillan, 1958.

Peridicals Consulted

Actualidad Militar
Caretas
El Comercio
La Crónica
Expreso
Latin America (London)
La Nación
Normas Legales: Revista de Legislación y Jurisprudencia
Oiga
The Peruvian Times
La Prensa
SINAMOS Informa
La Tribuna
Ultima Hora

Index

179

Third World countries, 136–37; authoritarian gains in, 7; democratization thesis for, 6–8; squatter "threat to sovereignty" in 41; urbanization figures for, 28
"Town in formation" (*pueblo en formación*), 19, 76
Trade policy, 15, 66, 67
Traficante, 75
Transportation, 112. *See also* Highway construction
Trujillo, 99
Trujillo Molina, Rafael Leonidas, 7
Tullock, Gordon, 71
Turner, John F. C., 42, 75
Twenty-Seventh of October settlement, 61, 64, 69, 88, 91

Uchumayo, 74
Ultima Hora (newspaper), 68, 69, 70, 76
Underemployment, urban, 3, 29
Unemployment, urban, 3, 23, 29
United States: land policies, compared with Peru, 53; tariff policy, 122–23
Urban commercial elite, 66–67, 127, 129, 132
Urban guerilla movement, specter of, 95, 96, 108, 121
Urbanización clandestina ("clandestine housing development"), 19
Urbanizaciónes populares ("lower-class housing projects"), 85–87, 88, 90, 105; discontinued, 115
Urbanization, 3, 6, 12, 14–15, 17, 31–34, 38, 67, 125; alternative policies to, 34, 81, 89, 115–16, 118; as cause of settlement formation, 27, 33; disruptive potential of, unrealized in Lima, 31–33, 121; housing statistics on, 28–29; under Odría, 63, 69, 80, 131; public policy regarding, under Belaúnde, 89, 115; public policy regarding, under Beltrán, 80–81; as result of settlement formation, 27, 33–34, 63, 125; statistics on, 15, 27–28; under Velasco, 115–16, 119
Urban reform, 116–18
Urban renewal, 36

Urban subsistence economy, 30
Uruguay, 7
U.S. Agency for International Development, 99

Velasco Alvarado, General Juan, 22, 95, 102, 103, 110
Velasco government, 92, 95–124, 127–28, 132; agrarian reform program of, 96, 107, 115, 118; concern of, with law, 96, 101, 113–15, 121; economic policy of, 107; housing policy of, 100, 104, 115, 118; land policies of, 101, 111, 113–16, 117, 118, 121–22; Law 17803 of 1969, 118, 122; ONDEPJOV program, 97–100, 101, 103–4; policy failures of, 113, 123–24; policy of, toward urbanization, 115–16, 119; political hierarchism of, 106–9, 120, *table* 129, 130; role of military in, 95–96, 97, 98, 102, 108–9, 132; role of, in settlement, 81, 97–104, 106–16, 118–24, 129, 130, 132; self-help philosophy of, 98–99, 100, 107, 111, 119, 120, 129, 130; settlement statistics on, 48, *table* 49, *tables* 151–52; SINAMOS program, 106–15, 120, 123; squatter evictions under, *table* 50, 102, 104, 113–14; and urban reform, 116–18
Venezuela, 51, 133
Vía legal, 115, 123
Villa el Salvador, 104, 109, 110, 111–12, 113, 115, 116, 121, 123
Voter statistics, 15, *table* 144; voter participation in settlements vs. slums, 25

Water supply, 21, 23, 112
Welfare policies, 134–35
Working classes, 10, 12–13, 55, 58, 96; and homeownership ideal, 77–78, 130; mobilization of, in Peru, compared with other nations, 133–34

"Young towns" (*pueblos jóvenes*), 19, 97–98, 99

Zoning requirements, 29, 76

THE JOHNS HOPKINS UNIVERSITY PRESS

This book was composed in Times Roman text and display type
by Jones Composition Company, and printed on Warren's 50-lb.
Publisher's Eggshell Wove paper. It was printed and bound by
Universal Lithographers, Inc.

Library of Congress Cataloging in Publication Data

Collier, David, 1942–
   Squatters and oligarchs.

   Bibliography: pp. 169–78.
   Includes index.
   1. Squatters—Lima. 2. Land settlement—Lima.
I. Title.
HD555.C65   333.1′0985′2   75-34112
ISBN 0-8018-1748-X